Don't Believe Everything You Imagine

Break Free from Limiting Beliefs and Transform Your Life

Martha Boyd

Dedication

To every soul who has ever felt trapped by their thoughts, weighed down by self-doubt, or lost in the endless cycles of overthinking—this book is for you.

To the ones who have cried in silence, questioning their worth, and to those who have woken up every day fighting battles no one else can see, your resilience is nothing short of extraordinary.

To the dreamers who dare to imagine a life beyond fear, the fighters who refuse to give up even when it feels impossible, and the seekers yearning for clarity, peace, and freedom—your courage inspires this work.

And to those who feel broken and overwhelmed, know that you are not alone. You are worthy of joy, capable of change, and deserving of a life unburdened by the weight of your mind.

This book is my offering to you—a guide, a companion, and a reminder that transformation is not only possible but waiting for you with open arms. May it light your path toward the peace and freedom you've always deserved.

COPYRIGHT

Copyright © 2024 by [Martha Boyd]

All rights reserved. No part of this book may be reproduced, distributed, or transmitted in any form or by any means, including photocopying, recording, or other electronic or mechanical methods, without the prior written permission of the author, except in the case of brief quotations embodied in critical reviews and certain other noncommercial uses permitted by copyright law.

Why This Book

Have you ever felt trapped by your thoughts, as if your mind is an endless loop of self-doubt, anxiety, and limiting beliefs? Do you find yourself questioning whether you'll ever truly break free from the mental barriers holding you back? What if the key to living the life you've always dreamed of lies not in doing more, but in thinking differently?

This book is for anyone who feels burdened by the weight of their own imagination, caught in cycles of overthinking, or paralyzed by the fear of change. It's a guide for those seeking transformation—not through fleeting motivation, but through lasting clarity and inner peace.

What This Book Offers

This isn't just another self-help book filled with clichés and temporary fixes. *Don't Believe Everything You Imagine: Break Free from Limiting Beliefs and Transform Your Life* goes deeper, addressing the root causes of your struggles and providing actionable strategies to help you:

- Identify and release the limiting beliefs that keep you stuck.

- Overcome overthinking, anxiety, and self-doubt without relying on sheer willpower.

- Cultivate emotional resilience to handle life's uncertainties with confidence.

- Reimagine success and happiness on your terms, free from societal pressures.
- Develop practical daily habits for mental clarity, inner peace, and long-term growth.

This book combines practical techniques, thought-provoking insights, and relatable examples, making it both transformative and easy to apply to your daily life.

Why This Book Matters to You

Imagine a life where you're no longer a prisoner of your mind, where you can confidently pursue your dreams, and where your inner peace is no longer dependent on external circumstances. The strategies in this book have been meticulously designed to guide you toward that reality. By turning the page, you'll discover:

- Why the stories you tell yourself shape your reality—and how to rewrite them.
- A three-step process to break free from overthinking and achieve mental clarity.
- How to discern between fear and wisdom, so you can make decisions with confidence.
- The secrets to finding unconditional joy, even in challenging times.

What Makes This Book Different

Unlike many self-help books that only scratch the surface, this book delves into the psychology of limiting beliefs and provides tangible tools for lasting change. It's grounded in empathy, actionable advice, and a deep understanding of the challenges you face.

Maybe you're skeptical. Maybe you've tried other methods and feel like nothing works. That's okay. This book doesn't promise perfection—it offers a fresh perspective and proven strategies that have helped countless others reclaim their lives.

Your Journey Begins Here

Your current struggles don't define you, and your thoughts don't have to control your life. The solutions you've been searching for are within these pages. Let this book guide you to a life of clarity, confidence, and transformation.

Keep reading. The answers to your most pressing questions—and the tools to break free—are waiting for you.

Table of Contents

INTRODUCTION 9

    WHY YOU'RE NOT ALONE IN YOUR STRUGGLE 13

    THE PROMISE OF THIS BOOK 16

    A FRESH WAY TO BREAK FREE 19

CHAPTER 1: WHAT WE IMAGINE SHAPES OUR REALITY 25

    THE INVISIBLE POWER OF BELIEFS 29

    HOW OUR MINDS CREATE SUFFERING 32

CHAPTER 2: THE CYCLE OF LIMITING BELIEFS 37

    WHY WE HOLD ONTO FALSE NARRATIVES 40

    IDENTIFYING THE STORIES THAT HOLD YOU BACK 44

CHAPTER 3: OVERTHINKING AND ITS COSTS 49

    THE HIDDEN TOLL OF MENTAL SPIRALS 52

    WHEN IMAGINATION TURNS AGAINST YOU 55

CHAPTER 4: DEBUNKING THE MYTHS ABOUT THINKING 61

    WHY POSITIVE THINKING ALONE ISN'T ENOUGH 64

    THE ILLUSION OF OVER-CONTROL 67

CHAPTER 5: RECLAIMING YOUR MENTAL FREEDOM 71

    PRACTICAL STRATEGIES TO BREAK THE CYCLE 74

    THE THREE-STEP PROCESS TO LET GO OF OVERTHINKING 77

CHAPTER 6: HOW TO RECOGNIZE AND REPLACE LIMITING BELIEFS ... 81

    TOOLS FOR CHALLENGING FALSE ASSUMPTIONS 84

TURNING SELF-DOUBT INTO EMPOWERMENT 87

CHAPTER 7: THE ROLE OF INTUITION IN EVERYDAY DECISIONS 91

TRUSTING YOUR GUT WHILE AVOIDING BIAS 94

HOW TO DIFFERENTIATE FEAR FROM WISDOM 97

CHAPTER 8: REIMAGINING SUCCESS AND HAPPINESS 101

WHY YOUR GOALS NEED A FRESH PERSPECTIVE 104

REDEFINING FULFILLMENT ON YOUR TERMS..107

CHAPTER 9: BUILDING EMOTIONAL RESILIENCE 111

LETTING GO OF ANXIETY AND SELF-DOUBT..114

HOW TO NAVIGATE LIFE'S UNCERTAINTY WITH GRACE 117

CHAPTER 10: FROM FEAR TO FREEDOM 123

USING CHALLENGES TO UNLOCK PERSONAL GROWTH 126

HOW TO FACE LIFE'S UNKNOWNS WITH CONFIDENCE................................130

CHAPTER 11: DAILY PRACTICES FOR MENTAL CLARITY 135

JOURNALING PROMPTS TO REFRAME YOUR THOUGHTS 138

MINDFULNESS TECHNIQUES FOR EMOTIONAL BALANCE 142

CHAPTER 12: LETTING GO AND LIVING IN THE PRESENT 147

HOW TO STOP WORRYING ABOUT THE PAST OR FUTURE...........................150

EMBRACING SIMPLICITY FOR INNER PEACE 153

CHAPTER 13: THE PATH TO UNCONDITIONAL JOY 157

CREATING A MINDSET OF ABUNDANCE AND FLOW 160

FINDING PEACE REGARDLESS OF CIRCUMSTANCES....................................163

CONCLUSION: YOUR JOURNEY BEGINS HERE **167**

    LIVING WITH AWARENESS AND INTENTION 170

    HOW TO SUSTAIN CHANGE AND CONTINUE GROWING 173

Introduction

It started with a phone call.

My friend, Joan, had always been the type of person who appeared to have it all together. She was a successful architect, happily married, with two beautiful kids. But the voice on the other end of the line that day was different. Broken.

Her voice barely a whisper, she asked, 'Do you ever feel trapped in your head?'

She went on to explain how her thoughts had become relentless critics—telling her she wasn't enough, warning her of disasters that never came, and replaying past mistakes like a broken record. Despite her achievements, she couldn't escape the feeling that something was wrong. "I've tried everything," she confessed. "Therapy, meditation, self-help books, and even those late-night webinars about manifesting your dream life. But nothing sticks. It feels like I'm in a battle I'm destined to lose."

That phone call wasn't just a turning point for Joan—it was a wake-up call for me too. I realized how many of us live with the same invisible struggle: an internal war waged by our thinking. The cruel irony? The very tool we rely on to solve problems—our minds—often becomes the source of our deepest suffering.

It's not just Joan. Maybe you've felt it too.

You've found yourself lying awake at night, replaying a conversation, worrying about the future, or doubting your decisions. Or perhaps you've felt stuck, unable to move forward because your thoughts keep circling back to "What if?" or "Why me?"

Here's the truth most people don't realize: **The mind is a powerful storyteller—but not all its stories are true.**

This book isn't just about recognizing the lies we tell ourselves. It's about breaking free from them.

At some point, we all come to a crossroads: continue believing the narratives our minds create or challenge them to discover a deeper, freer way of living. Most of the suffering we experience—self-doubt, anxiety, perfectionism, even fear of failure—can be traced back to one culprit: **our unchecked imagination.**

What if I told you there's a solution? What if I told you that you could quiet the noise in your head, let go of limiting beliefs, and finally live with the freedom, joy, and peace you've always been searching for?

This isn't about positive thinking or plastering affirmations over the cracks in your self-esteem. It's not about trying harder or pushing through with sheer willpower. Instead, this book offers a new way of seeing—a way to recognize and release the mental habits that keep you trapped.

By the time you finish this book, you'll understand:

- Why our imagination is both a blessing and a curse—and how to use it wisely.
- The subtle ways limiting beliefs sneak into your life and hold you back.
- How to stop overthinking, even when it feels impossible.
- Why you don't need to change who you are to transform your life.

More importantly, you'll gain the tools to break free from your mental chains—not through struggle, but through insight.

This book is divided into four parts:

1. **The Root of the Problem**: We'll uncover why our minds are so good at creating suffering and how to identify the limiting beliefs that keep us stuck.

2. **Breaking Free**: You'll learn practical, step-by-step strategies to challenge and replace those beliefs.

3. **Creating a Life Beyond Limits**: We'll explore how to cultivate resilience, embrace uncertainty, and find joy in the present moment.

4. **Tools for Transformation**: Finally, I'll share daily practices and exercises to help you sustain these changes and live with clarity and purpose.

Let me address some common concerns.

- **This is not about "thinking positive."** While optimism has its place, this book goes deeper, showing you how to work with your thoughts, not against them.

- **This isn't another mindfulness 101 guide.** While mindfulness is powerful, what I'll share here will help you go beyond meditation and into practical, everyday transformation.

- **This isn't one-size-fits-all advice.** Whether you're a high achiever, someone dealing with trauma, or simply tired of feeling stuck, this book meets you where you are.

The biggest breakthrough you'll experience might surprise you: You don't have to "fix" yourself to find peace. You're not broken. The real you—the one beneath all the overthinking, doubt, and fear—has always been there, waiting to emerge.

If you've ever felt like your mind is both your greatest gift and your greatest enemy, this book was written for you. Let's rewrite the story together.

Are you ready to let go of the lies and discover the truth of who you are?

Why You're Not Alone in Your Struggle

It might feel like you're the only one stuck in this endless loop of overthinking but let me assure you: you're not. In fact, the very reason you're holding this book in your hands is proof of something bigger—you're part of a quiet, unseen struggle that millions of people are experiencing every single day. You're not broken. You're not defective. And you're definitely not alone.

We live in a world where the mind has become both our most powerful ally and our greatest tormentor. Our ability to imagine, analyze, and dream is what allows us to create art, solve problems, and build lives we're proud of. But that same imagination, when left unchecked, can turn into a runaway train, carrying us down tracks of fear, self-doubt, and endless "what ifs." It's a paradox: the mind that's capable of such beauty and brilliance can also be the source of our deepest pain.

Have you ever wondered why your thoughts feel so loud sometimes, as if they're shouting over everything else? Or why, no matter how much you achieve or how much reassurance you get, that nagging voice in your head finds a way to make you feel small, unworthy, or uncertain? That's the mind's favorite trick: it convinces you that your thoughts are facts. But thoughts aren't truths—they're interpretations, guesses, and often, outright fabrications. They don't define you, and they certainly don't have to control you.

Whether it's perfectionism, self-doubt, or the never-ending churn of anxious thoughts, the mind often convinces us that the only way out is through more thinking. Once I figure this out, I'll feel better. If I just plan everything perfectly, nothing will go wrong. If I just keep replaying this moment in my head, I'll finally make sense of it. But the harder we think, the deeper we sink. It's like trying to escape quicksand by flailing—the more you fight, the faster you're pulled under.

What if I told you there's another way? A way to live where your thoughts no longer dictate your emotions, your actions, or your self-worth. A way to let go of the endless mental chatter and reconnect with the peace and clarity that's always been within you. This isn't some abstract, feel-good promise—it's something tangible, something you can practice and experience for yourself. The great thing is, you already possess everything necessary to break free. The bad news? The mind will fight back.

The mind thrives on control. It likes to predict, categorize, and solve. But what it doesn't understand—what it can't grasp—is that some of life's most profound truths aren't meant to be understood. They are intended to be felt, experienced, and lived. That's why this book isn't about giving you more concepts to memorize or strategies to overanalyze. It's about showing you how to move beyond your thinking, to a space where imagination serves you instead of sabotaging you.

Now, I know what you might be thinking. "This sounds wonderful, but what about my actual problems? My bills, my relationships, my responsibilities? How can I possibly stop overthinking when there's so much to figure out?" That's the mind again, trying to convince you that freedom is out of reach, that peace can only come once you've solved every problem in your life. But here's the truth: peace doesn't come from solving all your problems. It comes from realizing that you don't have to solve everything. Some of the greatest breakthroughs happen not because we figured something out, but because we let go of the need to figure it out at all.

By the time you reach the next page, you'll understand why this isn't about willpower or motivation. Those tools are like trying to build a house with a hammer when what you really need is a blueprint. This is about shifting the way you see your mind, your thoughts, and ultimately, yourself. It's about giving you the tools to create a life that isn't ruled by fear or doubt but guided by clarity and purpose.

What's coming next? I'll share the promise of this book—not just what you'll learn, but how it will fundamentally change the way you experience your life. The journey we're about to take together isn't just about reading words on a page. It's about reclaiming your power, one thought at a time.

The Promise of This Book

If you've made it this far, it's because something deep inside you already knows there has to be more to life than the constant noise in your head. You've tried the advice that promises quick fixes—"just think positively," "just push through," "just ignore the negative thoughts"—and yet, here you are, still searching. That's because most advice doesn't address the root of the problem. It's like slapping a bandage over a wound without stopping to ask why you're bleeding in the first place.

The promise of this book is simple but profound: by the time you finish reading, you will no longer be at the mercy of your imagination. You'll see clearly how your mind has been constructing your reality and how you can gently—but powerfully—reshape it. This isn't about giving you one more thing to "try harder" at. It's about helping you experience a shift so transformative that your mind stops being your master and becomes the supportive tool it was always meant to be.

Imagine waking up in the morning and not being greeted by the same spiral of anxious thoughts. Imagine no longer overanalyzing every word you said in a conversation or replaying that one embarrassing moment from years ago.

Imagine being able to move through your day with a sense of clarity, knowing that you are enough exactly as you are—not because of what you achieve, not because of what others think, but because the deepest part of you is whole and complete already.

This isn't just theoretical. It's real, and it's possible for you. But here's the thing: it doesn't require years of work or the perfect set of circumstances. You don't need to quit your job, move to a mountaintop, or spend hours meditating. The freedom I'm talking about comes from a shift in how you relate to your thoughts—a shift that can happen in an instant, though its effects will last a lifetime.

Let me be clear: this book isn't about forcing yourself to stop thinking. That approach would only create more tension, more resistance, and more frustration. What we're aiming for is a release—a softening of the grip your thoughts have on you. It's like relaxing a tightly closed hand. You've been holding on so tightly to your beliefs, your fears, and your mental habits that you haven't stopped to notice that letting go is even an option.

One of the greatest truths you'll discover in these pages is this: not every thought deserves your attention. Thoughts may arise, but they don't have to define you. The moment you realize that you can observe your thoughts without being swept away by them is the moment you begin to reclaim your power.

This isn't a promise of a perfect life. Challenges will still come, and difficult emotions will still arise. But the difference is that you won't feel controlled by them. You'll discover how to respond instead of reacting. You'll find that peace and clarity aren't things you have to chase—they're already here, waiting for you to notice them.

Throughout this journey, I'll guide you through actionable steps to break free from limiting beliefs and overthinking. You'll learn how to gently question the stories your mind tells you and replace them with truths that empower rather than hinder you. You'll uncover the role of intuition and how it can become your compass in life, steering you toward decisions that feel aligned with your deepest values. And you'll discover daily practices that don't feel like chores but like invitations to step into a freer, more authentic version of yourself.

But more importantly, this book will challenge you to see the world—and yourself—in a completely new way. You'll begin to notice the space between your thoughts, the quiet stillness that's been there all along. In that space, you'll find not only peace but also the clarity to create a life that feels meaningful and fulfilling.

Here's the truth: you don't need fixing. You don't need to become someone else. The freedom you're looking for isn't out there—it's already within you. What this book will do is help you uncover it, step by step, until you realize you've had the power to break free all along.

I know you might be skeptical. You might be thinking, "I've tried books like this before, and they didn't work for me." That's understandable. But here's what makes this journey different: it's not about adding more to your plate. It's about subtracting. Letting go. Simplifying. It's about finding freedom not by doing more, but by doing less—less overthinking, less resisting, less fighting against yourself.

As we step into the next chapter, I'll show you a fresh way to approach your thoughts and emotions—one that doesn't rely on motivation, willpower, or endless effort. This shift will change not just how you think, but how you experience life itself. And once you feel it, you'll wonder how you ever lived any other way.

For now, take a deep breath. The journey ahead isn't about fixing what's broken. It's about discovering what's been whole and unshakable all along. When you're ready, let's keep going. Your life is waiting.

A Fresh Way to Break Free

Imagine for a moment that you're standing in front of a door. On the other side lies the freedom you've been searching for—the ability to live without being weighed down by your own thoughts, to wake up each day and feel at ease, and to make choices guided by clarity and not fear. The key to this door is in your hand. But here's the catch: it doesn't open by force. It opens by understanding.

That's what this book is about—not pushing harder, thinking more, or piling on another set of strategies to your already-overwhelmed mind. It's about showing you how to use the key you've been holding all along. This isn't another method that will require constant effort to maintain. It's a fresh way of seeing, a shift that can change how you experience life at its very core.

Most approaches to personal growth ask you to fight your thoughts or force yourself into new ones. They tell you to "be positive" or "let it go," as if the solution were as simple as flipping a switch. But the mind doesn't work that way. If you've tried these approaches, you've probably felt the tension of trying to force your way out of overthinking, only to end up feeling more stuck. That's because the harder you fight your thoughts, the stronger they become.

What if, instead of fighting, you simply stepped back?

A fresh way to break free isn't about battling your mind—it's about befriending it. It starts with recognizing that your thoughts aren't your enemies, even the difficult ones. They're just mental events passing through, like clouds in the sky. Some are light and fluffy, others are stormy and dark, but none of them define the sky itself. Here's the truth: you are not the clouds. You are the sky.

When you begin to see your thoughts this way, something remarkable happens. The grip they've had on you starts to loosen. The stories they tell lose their power. You stop identifying with every fear, doubt, or assumption that passes through your mind. And in that space—between you and your thoughts—you discover a freedom that no external achievement or change in circumstances could ever bring.

But how do you get there? This book will help you find the answer to that question.

A fresh way to break free involves stepping outside the mental loops you've been caught in for so long. It's about shifting your focus from trying to fix the content of your thoughts to understanding the nature of your thinking itself. Rather than asking, "How do I stop feeling this way?" you'll learn to ask, "What's fueling these thoughts in the first place?" Once the answer becomes clear, the cycle starts to fade away.

For example, think about a time when you felt consumed by worry. Maybe you replayed a situation over and over, imagining all the ways it could go wrong. The worry felt real, pressing, undeniable. But was it the situation itself causing your distress, or was it your mind's interpretation of it? Most of the time, we're not reacting to life as it is—we're reacting to the stories our minds create about life.

This book offers a way to step outside those stories. It's not about suppressing your emotions or pretending that everything is fine. It's about learning to see your thoughts for what they are—temporary, changeable, and often unreliable. Once you do, the weight they carry begins to lift.

You'll also discover that breaking free doesn't mean giving up your dreams or ambitions. On the contrary, when your mind is no longer bogged down by overthinking and self-doubt, you'll find it easier to pursue what truly matters to you. You'll learn to trust your intuition, make decisions with confidence, and embrace life's uncertainties with a sense of curiosity rather than fear.

This isn't to say the process will be effortless. There will be moments when your old patterns resurface, when the pull of overthinking feels strong. But as you'll see in the chapters ahead, even these moments are opportunities for growth. Each time you catch yourself slipping back into the mental loop, you'll have the chance to practice letting go again—and each time you do, you'll feel a little lighter, a little freer.

The journey we're about to take is one of discovery, not just about your mind but about who you are beyond your thoughts. As you move through this book, you'll uncover truths that may surprise you: that you're not as stuck as you think, that you're more resilient than you realize, and that the peace you've been searching for has been within you all along.

In the next chapter, we'll dive into the root of the problem. You'll begin to see how the mind constructs your reality and why it feels so convincing.

More importantly, you'll learn how to start unravelling these mental constructs in a way that's both gentle and empowering. This is where the shift begins—where you stop living at the mercy of your imagination and start creating a life that feels truly free.

Take a deep breath. That door is closer than you think. And the key? You've already got it in your hand. Let's open it together.

Chapter 1: What We Imagine Shapes Our Reality

Our imagination is a double-edged sword. On one hand, it's the source of humanity's greatest achievements—art, innovation, and problem-solving. On the other, it's the root of so much of our unnecessary suffering. The way we interpret the world, the stories we tell ourselves, and the assumptions we make all stem from our imagination. What you imagine doesn't just stay in your head; it shapes how you see reality, how you react to it, and ultimately, the life you live.

Recall a moment when you were certain something negative was about to occur. Maybe it was an important meeting, and you imagined fumbling over your words or saying something embarrassing. Perhaps it was a conversation with a loved one, and you were sure they'd misunderstand you or get upset. How much energy did you spend worrying about those scenarios? Did they feel real, as if they'd already happened? And when the moment finally arrived, did things unfold the way your mind predicted—or was the reality far different?

This is the subtle yet powerful trap of the imagination. What we think might happen often feels just as real as what's actually happening. And the more vivid the picture, the more it affects us emotionally. It's no wonder that anxiety, self-doubt, and fear can take such a hold on us—they're fueled not by reality, but by what we imagine reality to be.

But here's the kicker: your imagination isn't just passively interpreting the world around you. It's actively shaping your experience of it. What you focus on grows. If you walk into a room expecting rejection, you're more likely to notice the people who seem uninterested. If you approach a situation with dread, your body responds as if that fear were already justified—your heart races, your stomach tightens, and your mind goes into overdrive. In a very real sense, what you imagine becomes your reality.

This isn't just a psychological quirk; it's a feature of how the human brain works. Neuroscientists have found that the brain doesn't differentiate much between what you vividly imagine and what you actually experience. That's why a scary thought can make your palms sweat or an embarrassing memory can make your face flush, even though neither is happening in the present moment. Your brain reacts to what you feed it, whether it's true or not.

This is where many of us get stuck. We assume that our imagination is showing us the truth, but in reality, it's often creating a distorted picture. This isn't your fault. The mind evolved to anticipate danger and solve problems, which means it's naturally wired to imagine worst-case scenarios. This was useful when our ancestors needed to be hyper-alert to predators, but in today's world, it means we spend far too much time bracing for threats that don't exist.

Understanding this dynamic is the first step toward freedom. Once you realize that your imagination is not an impartial observer but an active participant in shaping your reality, you can begin to take back control. Instead of automatically believing the stories your mind creates, you can choose to question them. You can choose to focus on possibilities that empower you instead of those that paralyze you. And you can start to live from a place of clarity rather than fear.

Let me share a story to bring this idea to life. A man named Daniel once came to me feeling completely stuck. He was in his mid-thirties, smart, hardworking, and deeply unhappy. Every day, his mind told him the same story: "You're a failure. You should have done more by now. Everyone else is ahead of you." These thoughts consumed him, dictating his actions and robbing him of any sense of joy. He avoided social events because he didn't want to answer questions about his career. He stayed in a job he hated because he was afraid to take risks. His imagination had created a prison, and he didn't even realize he was the one holding the keys.

When Daniel began to examine his thoughts, something shifted. He started to see that the story in his head wasn't the truth—it was just one version of the truth, crafted by his fear of failure. He began to challenge those thoughts: Was he really a failure, or was he just comparing himself to an impossible standard? Was it true that everyone else was ahead of him, or was he cherry-picking examples to confirm his insecurities?

Little by little, he learned to separate his thoughts from reality. And as he did, his world began to change. He took steps toward a career that excited him. He reconnected with old friends. He found himself laughing more, worrying less, and living in a way that felt authentic.

Daniel's story isn't unique. We all carry around mental narratives that shape how we see ourselves and the world. The good news is that these narratives aren't set in stone. They're created by our imagination, which means they can be reimagined.

In the chapters ahead, we'll dive deeper into how these mental stories form and why they hold so much power over us. We'll explore the invisible beliefs that keep us stuck and learn how to dismantle them, piece by piece. The next step is to uncover the invisible power of beliefs—the quiet forces that shape your reality without you even realizing it. Once you see these beliefs for what they are, you'll understand just how much power you have to rewrite the script.

Your mind has been shaping your reality all along. Isn't it time you took the pen back? Turn the page, and let's keep going. The life you've dreamed of, full of freedom and opportunities, is nearer than you realize.

The Invisible Power of Beliefs

Beliefs are powerful, not because they are inherently true, but because we treat them as if they are. They shape how we interpret the world, how we respond to challenges, and even what we think we deserve in life. The tricky part? Most of the beliefs driving our behavior aren't ones we consciously chose. They were absorbed, adopted, and reinforced over time—quietly becoming the invisible framework of our reality.

Think about this: every decision you make, every fear you feel, and every goal you set is influenced by your beliefs. They serve as lenses that shape how you view the world. But here's the thing about lenses: they can distort as much as they can clarify. If your beliefs are rooted in fear, self-doubt, or scarcity, they color your world in ways that limit you. Suddenly, opportunities look like risks, challenges seem insurmountable, and joy feels like something reserved for other people.

One of the reasons beliefs are so powerful is that they operate in the background, often without us realizing it. You might think you're just reacting to life as it is, but more often than not, you're reacting to your interpretation of life—a story shaped by your beliefs. For example, if you believe that success only comes through struggle, you might sabotage opportunities that feel too easy.

If you believe that you're unworthy of love, you might find yourself pushing people away, even when they care for you deeply.

Here's a truth that's both liberating and unsettling: beliefs aren't facts. They're conclusions your mind has drawn, often based on limited information or past experiences. And yet, because we treat them as truths, they become self-fulfilling. If you believe the world is full of rejection, you'll unconsciously look for evidence to support that belief—and you'll find it, not because it's true, but because your mind is wired to confirm what it already believes.

Let's take a step deeper. Many of our core beliefs are formed during childhood, a time when our minds are like sponges, soaking up everything around us. These beliefs often originate from the people closest to us—parents, teachers, friends—who were themselves shaped by their own beliefs. Maybe you were told, directly or indirectly, that you needed to work harder to be loved. Or that it wasn't safe to trust others. Or that failure was something to avoid at all costs. Over time, these messages settled into your subconscious, quietly influencing how you see yourself and the world.

The problem isn't that we have beliefs. It's that we rarely stop to question them. We don't ask where they came from, whether they're still relevant, or whether they were ever true in the first place. And so, they remain, shaping our choices and experiences without our awareness. The good news is that once you recognize your beliefs, you have the ability to change them.

Changing a belief isn't about forcing yourself to think differently. It's about gently questioning the assumptions you've been living by. Start by asking yourself: Is this belief serving me? Is it helping me grow, or is it keeping me stuck? If it's the latter, ask yourself another question: What evidence do I have that this belief is true? You'll often find that the evidence is shaky at best, built on isolated incidents or outdated perceptions.

For years, a lady I know personally believed she wasn't "good with people." This belief kept her from pursuing leadership roles, networking, or even forming deeper friendships. When we dug into where that belief came from, she realized it stemmed from a single experience in high school, where she'd stumbled over her words during a presentation. That moment, amplified by her self-consciousness, became the foundation of a belief she carried for decades. But when she saw it for what it was—a single event, not a universal truth—she began to let it go. Today, Maria leads a team at her company and thrives in social settings she once avoided.

This process of examining and challenging your beliefs is transformative because it opens up new possibilities. When you release a limiting belief, you make space for something new—something expansive, empowering, and true. But this isn't a one-time event. It's an ongoing practice, one that requires curiosity and self-compassion.

What beliefs are shaping your life right now? What stories are you telling yourself about who you are and what's possible for you?

If you can start to question even one of those stories, you've already begun the process of breaking free.

In the next section, we'll explore how these invisible beliefs, when left unchecked, create patterns of suffering. You'll see why some struggles feel so persistent and learn how to disrupt the cycle. For now, I want you to sit with this thought: your beliefs are not permanent. They are not facts. And the moment you begin to question them, you start to reclaim your power.

How Our Minds Create Suffering

Suffering begins in the mind, not in the world around us. While life will always bring challenges—disappointments, losses, and moments of uncertainty—how we respond to these experiences determines whether they pass like a fleeting storm or take root and grow into suffering. The mind, with all its complexity and creativity, has a way of turning passing discomfort into something far heavier. The question is: why?

The mind creates suffering because it thrives on control. It constantly interprets, judges, and labels everything we encounter. It asks, "What does this mean? What does this say about me? What can I do to fix it or stop it from happening again?"

While this instinct can be helpful for problem-solving, it often spirals into a loop of overthinking and overanalyzing. The result?

We don't just experience pain or disappointment; we add layers of fear, regret, and worry on top of it.

Imagine a simple example: you receive a short, curt message from a friend. Instead of brushing it off or seeking clarification, your mind leaps into action. "Did I do something wrong? Are they upset with me? Maybe I shouldn't have said that thing last week." Before you know it, your thoughts have created an entire narrative, complete with imagined motives and future consequences. The original event—a neutral, momentary interaction—becomes a source of stress, not because of what actually happened, but because of the meaning your mind assigned to it.

This is the mind's first trick: it confuses thoughts with facts. A passing worry, a fleeting doubt, or an imagined worst-case scenario takes on the weight of truth simply because we think it. The more we dwell on these thoughts, the more real they feel. And the more real they feel, the more they shape our emotions and actions.

The second way the mind creates suffering is by resisting what is. When we face a difficult situation, the mind often rebels against it. "This shouldn't be happening. It's not fair. It's not how things are supposed to be." This resistance creates tension, frustration, and a sense of powerlessness. Instead of working with reality, we end up fighting against it, which only deepens our pain.

Let's look at an example. Picture yourself caught in traffic while heading to a crucial meeting. The situation itself is neutral—cars are moving slowly, and you're not going anywhere fast. But your mind doesn't see it that way. It starts spinning: "Why is this happening? I should have left earlier. Now I'm going to look unprofessional. This always happens to me!" The traffic, which is out of your control, becomes a source of immense stress—not because of the cars, but because of the story your mind is telling about them.

The third way the mind contributes to suffering is through its attachment to outcomes. The mind likes certainty. It craves predictability and control, so it clings to specific ideas of how life should unfold. When reality doesn't align with these expectations, we feel disappointed, anxious, or even devastated. We don't suffer because life didn't go our way—we suffer because we were so attached to the idea that it should.

Take someone who applies for their dream job. They pour their energy into the application process, imagining the perfect future it will create. But when they don't get the job, their mind spirals: "I'll never have another chance like this. I'm not good enough. "My future is destroyed." While rejection is undoubtedly painful, it's the mind's fixation on a particular outcome that transforms that pain into suffering.

Recognizing how the mind creates suffering is a powerful first step because it gives us a choice.

Once you see the patterns—how your thoughts turn neutral events into problems, how resistance amplifies discomfort, and how attachment breeds anxiety—you can start to loosen their grip. You don't have to believe every thought or follow every mental narrative. You can let go of the stories that aren't serving you.

This doesn't mean suppressing your thoughts or pretending everything is fine. It means observing your mind with curiosity and compassion, noticing when it's spinning stories, and reminding yourself that you are not your thoughts. The mind will always do what it does—it's wired that way. But you can choose how much power you give it.

If this seems more challenging in practice, there's no need to worry. In the next chapter, we'll explore the cycle of limiting beliefs and how they reinforce these patterns of suffering. You'll learn to identify the hidden beliefs driving your thoughts and take the first steps toward breaking free from their hold. For now, remember this: suffering isn't inevitable. It's a pattern, one that begins in the mind. Like any pattern, it is possible to change it. Turn the page, and let's take the next step together.

Chapter 2: The Cycle of Limiting Beliefs

Limiting beliefs are like invisible threads, quietly weaving themselves into the fabric of your life until they dictate what you can and cannot do. They begin as tiny, almost imperceptible whispers in the back of your mind: "You're not good enough," "You'll never succeed," or "People can't be trusted." Over time, these whispers grow louder, becoming the soundtrack to your thoughts and the lens through which you see the world. What starts as a single, fleeting idea becomes a pattern—a cycle—that shapes your actions, your emotions, and ultimately, your reality.

The cycle of limiting beliefs often begins with an experience. Maybe it's a failure, a rejection, or a criticism that stings just a little too deeply. In that moment, your mind tries to make sense of what happened, and it does so by forming a belief. "I failed at this, so I must not be capable." "They rejected me, so I must not be worthy." These thoughts seem logical and protective—your mind attempts to guard you from future pain by forming conclusions about the world and your role in it.

But here's where the cycle takes hold: once a limiting belief is formed, it influences your behavior. If you believe you're not capable, you might avoid opportunities where you could fail. If you believe you're not worthy, you might shrink back in relationships, fearing rejection.

These actions—or lack of actions—then create results that seem to confirm the belief. You don't take the chance, so you never experience success. You hold back emotionally, so relationships feel distant. And so the cycle continues, tightening its grip with every turn.

Let's break this down with a real-life example. Think about someone who believes they're not good at public speaking. Maybe the belief started in high school, after a nerve-wracking presentation that didn't go as planned. That one event planted a seed: "I'm bad at this." Over time, the person avoids situations that require speaking in front of others. They decline opportunities, like leading a meeting or giving a toast, because the thought of failing feels unbearable. Because they never practice or put themselves out there, their skills don't improve. And when they're finally forced into a speaking situation, the lack of experience leads to more discomfort, reinforcing the belief. The cycle becomes self-perpetuating.

The most dangerous thing about this cycle is how convincing it feels. Each time a belief is reinforced, it seems more true, more unshakable. You start to mistake the cycle for reality itself, forgetting that it was a belief—not a fact—that set it into motion. And because the mind likes consistency, it seeks out evidence that aligns with the belief while ignoring anything that contradicts it. This is why limiting beliefs can feel so hard to break—they become the filters through which you see everything.

But the cycle isn't invincible. The moment you recognize it for what it is—a pattern, not a truth—you begin to weaken its power. Awareness is the first crack in the armor of any limiting belief. When you start to notice the ways your beliefs influence your actions and your actions reinforce your beliefs, you create space for something new. You stop living on autopilot and start questioning the scripts that have been running your life.

To break the cycle, you need to challenge it at every step. Start by identifying the belief at its core. What thought or assumption is driving your actions? Reflect on this: what is the origin of this belief? Is it based on one isolated experience, or has it been shaped by fear and repetition? Most importantly, ask: is this belief true? Not just "does it feel true," but "does it hold up under scrutiny?" Often, you'll find that limiting beliefs are built on shaky foundations—half-truths, misunderstandings, or outdated ideas that no longer serve you.

Once you've questioned the belief, it's time to disrupt the actions that keep the cycle alive. If you normally avoid situations that challenge your belief, try stepping into them with curiosity. If you usually retreat at the first sign of discomfort, experiment with staying a little longer. This isn't about forcing yourself into change but about gently testing the boundaries of what you think is possible. Each small step you take toward challenging a belief weakens its hold and creates evidence for a new, more empowering story.

The process isn't always comfortable. Limiting beliefs are deeply ingrained, and challenging them can stir up resistance. Your mind might fight back, trying to pull you into old patterns. But each time you choose to question rather than comply, you take a step toward freedom. And with practice, you'll find that the beliefs that once felt like unshakable truths begin to lose their weight.

The cycle of limiting beliefs doesn't have to define you. It's a pattern, and like all patterns, it can be changed. The first step is recognizing the cycle for what it is—a story your mind has been telling you, not the truth about who you are or what you're capable of. Once you see the cycle clearly, you can start to rewrite the script.

In the next section, we'll explore why we hold onto false narratives, even when they hurt us. You'll learn how these stories take root and why letting go can feel so difficult. But more importantly, you'll discover how to loosen their grip and make room for the truth of who you are. The next chapter is waiting to show you what's possible.

Why We Hold onto False Narratives

If false narratives cause so much pain and limit our potential, why do we hold onto them so tightly? The answer lies in the comfort they provide, even as they quietly chip away at our happiness. False narratives, no matter how harmful, offer a sense of familiarity.

They provide a structure for how we perceive ourselves and the world around us. And for many of us, that framework feels safer than stepping into the unknown.

Imagine you've believed for years that you're not good at relationships. Maybe you've told yourself, "I always mess things up," or "I'm just not meant to be loved." As painful as these beliefs are, they serve a purpose: they shield you from taking risks. If you believe relationships will always fail, you can avoid putting yourself in vulnerable situations. You can sidestep the discomfort of intimacy, the fear of rejection, and the possibility of heartache. Strangely, your false narrative becomes your armor.

But that armor comes at a cost. While it protects you from perceived threats, it also cuts you off from the very things you desire—connection, growth, and fulfillment. It keeps you stuck in a cycle where safety takes precedence over joy, and the walls you build to protect yourself become the barriers that hold you back.

False narratives also persist because they feel like the truth. The human mind craves consistency, and once a belief takes hold, your brain starts looking for evidence to support it. This is known as confirmation bias, and it's one of the reasons limiting beliefs can be so difficult to break. If you believe you're unworthy, you'll focus on moments that seem to validate that belief—a critical comment, a rejection, or a perceived failure—while ignoring or downplaying evidence to the contrary.

Over time, the belief feels more and more solid, even though it's built on selective perception.

Another reason we cling to false narratives is that they often serve as explanations for our pain. When life feels chaotic or unpredictable, the mind seeks meaning. It wants to understand why things happen the way they do, and in the absence of clear answers, it creates its own. "I didn't get the promotion because I'm not smart enough." "They left me because I wasn't good enough." These explanations are rarely kind or accurate, but they provide a sense of closure. They give us something to hold onto, even if that something is a lie.

Sometimes, false narratives are passed down to us. They aren't even ours to begin with. Maybe you grew up in a household where success was equated with struggle, and now you believe that anything worthwhile must be hard-earned. Or perhaps you were told that emotions are a sign of weakness, so you suppress your feelings and see vulnerability as a flaw. These inherited beliefs become part of your internal script, shaping how you see yourself and the world without you even realizing it.

But here's the truth: just because a belief feels familiar doesn't mean it's true. Just because it provides comfort doesn't mean it's serving you. And just because it's been with you for a long time doesn't mean it has to stay.

To let go of false narratives, you first have to recognize the role they're playing in your life. What are they protecting you from? What needs are they trying to meet? Often, these beliefs are attempts to shield you from pain or provide a sense of control in an unpredictable world. Understanding this can help you approach them with compassion rather than judgment. After all, these narratives didn't arise out of nowhere—they were your mind's way of coping with uncertainty, fear, or hurt. But now, they've outlived their purpose.

Letting go of a false narrative doesn't mean rejecting it outright. It means examining it, questioning its validity, and deciding whether it still aligns with the life you want to create. This process requires curiosity and courage. It asks you to step out of your comfort zone and into a space where new possibilities can emerge. But the reward is worth it: the freedom to live a life that's guided by truth, not fear.

As we move forward, we'll delve into how to identify the stories that are holding you back. You'll learn to uncover the beliefs that have been running beneath the surface and bring them into the light where they can no longer control you. These stories may feel deeply ingrained, but as you'll see, they are not who you are. They are merely patterns, and patterns can be altered.

Identifying the Stories That Hold You Back

If you've ever felt stuck, doubted yourself, or held back from pursuing what truly matters to you, it's almost certain that a hidden story is playing in the background. These stories—the ones that whisper "you're not enough," "you'll never succeed," or "it's too late for you"—aren't just thoughts. They are narratives that have quietly shaped your choices, actions, and view of the world for years, maybe even decades. But here's the key: they only have power because they've gone unchallenged. The first step in breaking free is to identify these stories for what they are: beliefs, not facts.

Identifying the stories that hold you back begins with paying attention. These narratives are often so ingrained that they feel like background noise—something you barely notice because it's always been there. But every story leaves clues, and if you listen closely, you'll start to see their fingerprints on your life. Think about the areas where you feel most stuck or uncertain. Is it in your relationships, your career, your self-esteem? Wherever you feel resistance, a story is usually at work.

To uncover these stories, start by looking at your patterns. What do you consistently avoid or struggle with? Do you find yourself withdrawing in relationships because you're afraid of being hurt? Do you procrastinate on your goals because deep down, you don't believe you'll succeed? These patterns aren't random—they're evidence of the beliefs driving your behavior.

Once you've identified a pattern, ask yourself: what is the underlying story here? For example, if you avoid conflict, the story might be, "If I stand up for myself, I'll lose the people I care about." If you hesitate to take risks, the story might be, "If I fail, everyone will see me as a failure." These stories often feel logical because they've been reinforced over time, but that doesn't make them true. The goal isn't to judge yourself for believing these stories; it's to shine a light on them so you can begin to question them.

Keeping a journal can be a highly effective tool in this process. Sit down and write about a situation where you felt stuck or held back. What were you thinking in that moment? What fears came up? As you write, you'll likely notice a recurring theme—a belief or assumption that fueled your hesitation. This is the story you're working to uncover.

Another way to identify your limiting stories is to listen to your self-talk. Pay attention to the words you use when you're feeling doubtful or overwhelmed. Are you saying to yourself, "I always make mistakes" or "That's just not who I am"? These phrases might seem harmless, but they reveal the narratives running beneath the surface. Once you become aware of them, you can start to challenge them.

Sometimes, the stories holding you back aren't even your own. They're stories you've absorbed from others—family, friends, society—that have become part of your internal script. Maybe you grew up hearing that success requires sacrificing your happiness, so now you equate hard work with struggle.

Or maybe someone once told you that you weren't talented, and you've carried that belief ever since. Recognizing these inherited stories can be liberating because it reminds you that you don't have to carry someone else's narrative anymore.

As you identify these stories, you'll begin to notice how much they've shaped your life. But awareness alone isn't enough to break free. The next step is to question these stories, to test their validity, and to rewrite them in a way that empowers you. This isn't about forcing yourself to think positively; it's about finding a version of the story that feels both true and supportive.

For example, if your story is "I'm not good at relationships," you might rewrite it as, "I'm learning how to build healthier connections." If your story is "I'm too old to start over," you might reframe it as, "It's never too late to pursue what matters to me." These new narratives don't have to be perfect—they just have to open the door to possibility.

Breaking free from limiting stories is a process, not a one-time event. There will be days when the old narratives resurface, whispering their doubts and fears. But each time you catch yourself believing them, you have the opportunity to choose differently. And with practice, those whispers will grow quieter, replaced by a voice that reflects your true potential.

In the next chapter, we'll dive deeper into one of the biggest contributors to these stories: overthinking.

You'll learn how the constant mental chatter keeps you trapped in old patterns and discover practical steps to quiet your mind and reclaim your peace. But for now, take a moment to reflect on the stories you've uncovered. These aren't just obstacles—they're invitations to grow, to question, and to create a life that feels authentic to who you truly are.

Chapter 3: Overthinking and Its Costs

Overthinking is like being stuck in a revolving door, endlessly spinning but never stepping out. It masquerades as a productive habit, convincing you that if you think just a little longer, just a little harder, you'll find the solution, avoid the mistake, or make the perfect decision. But the truth is, overthinking rarely leads to clarity—it leads to exhaustion. It's a loop that drains your energy and keeps you trapped in a state of uncertainty and self-doubt.

At its core, overthinking is the mind's attempt to control what feels uncontrollable. It thrives in moments of ambiguity, uncertainty, and fear. When you don't have all the answers, your mind fills the gap with endless scenarios, possibilities, and worst-case outcomes. The problem is, the more you analyze, the more overwhelming things seem. Instead of finding peace, you create a storm of mental clutter that drowns out your intuition and paralyzes you from taking action.

Think about the last time you couldn't stop thinking about something. Maybe it was a decision you had to make, like whether to take a new job or end a relationship. Or maybe it was a mistake you made, and you kept replaying it, dissecting every detail, trying to figure out what went wrong. Did all that thinking bring you closer to resolution, or did it leave you feeling stuck, second-guessing yourself at every turn?

Overthinking doesn't just steal your time—it robs you of your ability to be present.

When your mind is consumed with analyzing the past or worrying about the future, you miss what's happening right now. You might be sitting with a loved one, but instead of enjoying their company, your thoughts are elsewhere, replaying a conversation or imagining a problem that hasn't even happened. Over time, this mental habit erodes your relationships, your peace of mind, and your overall sense of well-being.

One of the most damaging aspects of overthinking is how it feeds fear. Every time you dwell on a potential problem, you give it power. Your mind magnifies the risk and minimizes your ability to handle it, creating a sense of helplessness. This is why overthinking often leads to procrastination. The more you think about something, the bigger and scarier it seems, until you convince yourself that you're not ready or capable of dealing with it.

Overthinking also has a way of distorting your perception. It makes small issues feel enormous and temporary setbacks seem permanent. It's like holding a magnifying glass over your problems, seeing every flaw and imperfection in vivid detail while losing sight of the bigger picture. This distorted view keeps you focused on what's wrong, making it difficult to see what's right or possible.

To break free from the grip of overthinking, you have to understand its root cause: the mind's need for control. Overthinking is your mind's way of trying to protect you, but in doing so, it traps you in a cycle of fear and inaction.

The solution isn't to suppress your thoughts or force yourself to stop thinking—it's to step back and observe your mind without getting caught up in its stories. When you create space between yourself and your thoughts, you begin to see them for what they are: passing mental events, not absolute truths.

One simple yet powerful practice is to ask yourself, "Is this helpful?" If you notice yourself slipping into overthinking, take a moment to pause and reflect. Are your thoughts bringing you closer to a solution or are they just adding to your stress If it's the latter, calmly shift your attention back to the present moment. You can't think your way into peace, but you can choose to let go of the thoughts that disrupt it.

Another effective strategy is to set boundaries with your mind. Permit yourself to think about a problem for a set amount of time—say, ten minutes—and then consciously shift your focus to something else. This practice helps you take control of your mental energy instead of letting your thoughts run unchecked.

Breaking the habit of overthinking takes practice and patience, but the reward is worth it. When you learn to quiet the mental noise, you create space for clarity, creativity, and inner peace. You free yourself from the endless loop of "what ifs" and "if onlys" and begin to trust in your ability to handle whatever comes your way.

In the next section, we'll explore the hidden toll of mental spirals—the way overthinking affects not just your mind, but your body, emotions, and relationships. You'll see why breaking free isn't just about feeling better—it's about reclaiming your life.

The Hidden Toll of Mental Spirals

Overthinking isn't just a mental habit—it's a full-body experience that affects your emotions, your physical health, and your relationships in ways you may not even realize. The toll it takes goes beyond the hours spent lost in thought; it shows up in how you feel about yourself, how you connect with others, and even how your body functions. While the mind spirals through endless loops of worry and doubt, the rest of you quietly pays the price.

One of the most immediate effects of overthinking is emotional exhaustion. When your thoughts are constantly churning, your brain is working overtime, even when there's no productive outcome. This mental overdrive drains your emotional reserves, leaving you feeling depleted, irritable, or on edge. You might notice yourself becoming more impatient with others or snapping at small inconveniences that wouldn't normally bother you. This isn't because you're a bad person—it's because your mind has been running on fumes, and there's little energy left for anything else.

Overthinking also amplifies emotions like anxiety and fear. When your mind fixates on potential problems, it triggers your body's stress response. Your heart races, your breathing becomes shallow, and your muscles tense up, as if preparing for a threat. But unlike a real danger that comes and goes, the imagined threats of overthinking linger, keeping your body in a constant state of alert. Over time, this chronic stress can lead to physical symptoms like headaches, digestive issues, and fatigue, as well as long-term health problems if left unchecked.

Have you ever noticed how hard it is to focus on the present when you're caught in a mental spiral? Overthinking pulls your attention away from what's happening here and now, making it difficult to fully engage with your surroundings. You might be physically present with a loved one, but your mind is somewhere else, replaying a conversation or worrying about tomorrow. This disconnect not only affects your ability to enjoy the moment but also creates distance in your relationships. When you're preoccupied with your own thoughts, it's harder to truly listen, connect, and be present for the people who matter to you.

Overthinking also has a sneaky way of eroding your self-confidence. When you analyze every decision, every action, and every word, you start to doubt yourself. Did I say the wrong thing? Did I make the right choice? Am I good enough? These questions can quickly spiral into a cycle of self-criticism that chips away at your sense of self-worth.

The more you overthink, the more you question yourself, and the more you question yourself, the harder it becomes to trust your instincts.

Perhaps the most insidious effect of overthinking is how it keeps you stuck. Instead of taking action, you spend your time thinking about all the possible outcomes, weighing every option, and imagining every worst-case scenario. While this might feel like you're being thorough, it often leads to paralysis. The more you think, the more overwhelming the decision feels, until you convince yourself that it's safer to do nothing at all. Over time, this inaction reinforces the very fears and doubts that started the cycle, leaving you trapped in a loop of hesitation and regret.

Breaking free from overthinking starts with recognizing the toll it's taking on your life. Pay attention to the moments when your thoughts feel like they're spiraling out of control. Notice how your body reacts—are your shoulders tense, your stomach in knots? Notice how your emotions shift—do you feel more anxious, frustrated, or disconnected? Recognizing this is the initial step toward making a change. You can't stop what you don't notice, and by bringing your mental spirals into the light, you take the first step toward interrupting them.

One practical way to disrupt overthinking is to ground yourself in the present moment. When you feel your thoughts spinning, pause and bring your attention to something tangible.

Pay attention to the sensation of your breath, the contact of your feet with the ground, or the surrounding sounds. These simple acts of mindfulness help anchor you in reality, pulling you out of the imaginary world your mind has created.

Another strategy is to practice self-compassion. Overthinking often comes from a place of fear or self-doubt, and responding to yourself with kindness can help break the cycle. Instead of criticizing yourself for overthinking, try acknowledging it without judgment: "I'm feeling overwhelmed right now, and that's okay. I don't have to have all the answers right now." This shift in perspective can help you approach your thoughts with curiosity rather than fear, creating space for change.

In the next section, we'll explore what happens when imagination turns against you—the ways your mind can create scenarios that feel so real, they shape your emotions and actions as if they've already happened. You'll learn how to recognize these mental traps and take back control, one thought at a time. You're already making progress, and each step brings you closer to the freedom you deserve..

When Imagination Turns Against You

Imagination is one of humanity's greatest gifts. It's what allows us to dream, create, and innovate. But when imagination turns against us, it can feel more like a curse. The same mental tool that builds visions of possibility can construct prisons of fear, anxiety, and self-doubt.

And the most insidious part? The scenarios we imagine can feel just as real as the world around us, triggering emotions and reactions as if they were already happening.

Consider this: your boss sends you an email with a vague subject line—"Let's discuss tomorrow." Instantly, your imagination takes over. You start replaying recent conversations, dissecting every word you've said in meetings, and conjuring up worst-case scenarios. Maybe you picture being called out for a mistake you didn't even realize you made. Or perhaps your mind jumps straight to fears of losing your job. Before you've even opened the email, your heart is racing, your palms are sweating, and you're bracing for a conversation that may not even happen.

This is the power of imagination turned inward. It pulls you into a mental movie, complete with vivid details and emotional weight, even though nothing has actually happened. Your mind creates a narrative, and your body responds as if it's true. This is why overthinking feels so exhausting—it's not just mental work; it's emotional and physical labor as well.

When imagination works against you, it doesn't just stop at worry. It creates cycles of avoidance and self-sabotage. For instance, let's say you've been invited to speak at an event. Your initial excitement quickly turns to dread as your imagination kicks in. You picture yourself fumbling through your words, the audience looking bored or even judgmental.

The fear grows, and before you know it, you've convinced yourself that it's better to decline the opportunity altogether. But in avoiding the imagined discomfort, you miss out on the real chance to grow and shine.

This pattern often starts with a single "what if." What if I fail? What if they don't like me? What if I can't handle it? While these questions may feel like they're preparing you for the worst, they're actually magnifying your fears. Each imagined scenario adds another layer of stress, pulling you further away from the present moment and deeper into a world of hypothetical suffering.

So, why does the mind do this? At its core, it's about survival. The brain is wired to predict and prepare for potential threats, a trait that was incredibly useful when those threats were predators or natural disasters. But in today's world, where most dangers are emotional or social, this survival mechanism can backfire. Instead of protecting you, it keeps you stuck in a cycle of over-analysis and fear, preventing you from living fully.

The good news is that imagination, even when it turns against you, isn't inherently bad. It's simply a tool—one that can be redirected to serve you rather than hinder you. The first step in regaining control is recognizing when your imagination is pulling you into a negative spiral. Pay attention to the stories your mind is creating. Are they based on facts, or are they assumptions and projections?

More often than not, you'll find that the scenarios you're dwelling on are rooted in fear rather than reality.

One way to disrupt this pattern is to challenge your imagined fears with curiosity. Ask yourself: What evidence do I have that this scenario will happen? Have I faced similar situations before, and how did they turn out? By bringing logic into the equation, you can start to poke holes in the mental narrative and reduce its grip on you.

Another powerful technique is to shift your focus from "what if" to "what is." Ground yourself in the present moment by tuning into your senses. What are you noticing, listening to, and experiencing at this moment? This simple practice can anchor you back to reality, breaking the cycle of imaginary catastrophes.

And finally, remember that your imagination can work for you, not just against you. Instead of picturing the worst, try visualizing positive outcomes. What if the meeting goes well? What if the audience loves your speech? By consciously choosing to imagine success, you can counterbalance the mind's tendency to dwell on fear and open yourself up to possibilities.

Imagination is a powerful force, but it doesn't have to control you. When you learn to recognize and redirect it, you reclaim your ability to live with clarity and confidence. The scenarios your mind creates are just that—scenarios.

They don't define you, and they don't dictate your future. Only you have the power to decide how much weight to give them.

In the next chapter, we'll begin to dismantle the myths about thinking that keep you trapped in cycles of over-analysis and doubt. You'll discover why more thinking isn't always the answer and learn strategies to quiet your mind and create space for peace. For now, let this be your reminder: your thoughts are not your enemy, and your imagination is not your master. Turn the page, and let's continue this journey of freedom together.

Chapter 4: Debunking the Myths About Thinking

We're taught to believe that thinking is the ultimate tool for solving problems, finding clarity, and improving our lives. From a young age, we're praised for our ability to "think things through" and encouraged to use our minds as the ultimate decision-making engine. But what if that belief isn't entirely true? What if, in some cases, thinking too much is the very thing holding you back from peace, growth, and freedom?

The first myth we need to challenge is that more thinking leads to better solutions. This idea seems logical on the surface—after all, careful thought is necessary for solving problems. But there's a tipping point where thinking shifts from productive to paralyzing. When you overanalyze, you don't gain clarity; you lose it. You start running the same scenarios over and over, hoping to find the perfect answer, only to feel more uncertain than when you started.

Think about a time when you were faced with a tough decision. Maybe you replayed every option, weighed every pro and con, and considered every possible outcome. Did the extra hours of analysis bring you closer to peace, or did they leave you feeling more stuck? Overthinking isn't about solving a problem—it's about trying to control the uncontrollable. The truth is, that many of life's decisions don't have a perfect answer, and no amount of thinking will eliminate the inherent uncertainty.

Another myth about thinking is that it's the only way to understand yourself. It's easy to fall into the trap of believing that if you can just think hard enough, you'll figure out why you feel the way you do or why certain patterns keep showing up in your life. But the mind isn't always the best tool for self-discovery. It can be biased, limited, and overly focused on problems. True understanding often comes from stillness, from creating space for your intuition and inner wisdom to surface. When you step out of the mental noise, you might be surprised at the clarity that emerges.

The third myth we need to address is that thinking protects you from failure. Many of us believe that if we think through every detail and anticipate every risk, we can avoid mistakes and disappointment. But this mindset creates a false sense of control. The truth is, that life is unpredictable, and no amount of planning can shield you from every possibility. Overthinking doesn't prevent failure; it prevents action. And without action, you miss out on the experiences that lead to growth and success.

One of the most harmful myths about thinking is that it defines who you are. Many of us identify so closely with our thoughts that we believe they are a reflection of our true selves. But your thoughts are not you. They are fleeting, ever-changing, and often influenced by fear, habit, or external factors. The moment you realize this—that you are the observer of your thoughts, not the thoughts themselves—is the moment you begin to reclaim your freedom.

So how do you start debunking these myths in your own life? It begins with awareness. Pay attention to the moments when your mind is working overtime. Are you analyzing a decision to the point of exhaustion? Are you trying to think your way out of an emotion? Are you stuck in a loop of self-doubt, believing that if you just think harder, you'll find the solution? Identifying these patterns is the initial step toward gaining freedom.

The next step is to evaluate how useful your thoughts are. Ask yourself: Is this line of thinking helping me, or is it keeping me stuck? Am I searching for an answer that doesn't exist, or am I avoiding the discomfort of uncertainty? By gently challenging your mind, you create space for new possibilities to emerge.

Finally, practice letting go of the need to think your way into peace. This doesn't mean shutting off your mind or avoiding thought altogether—it means recognizing when thinking has done its job and stepping back. Give yourself permission to rest, to be still, and to trust that not every problem needs a solution right now. Often, the clarity you're seeking comes when you stop chasing it.

Moving forward, we'll explore another common trap: the belief that positive thinking alone is enough to transform your life. You'll discover why trying to force positivity can sometimes do more harm than good and learn how to cultivate a mindset that's both realistic and empowering.

For now, take a moment to reflect on the myths you've uncovered about thinking. What would it feel like to loosen their grip and trust in something deeper? Let's continue this journey together.

Why Positive Thinking Alone Isn't Enough

Positive thinking is often hailed as the ultimate solution to life's challenges. The idea is simple: if you think positively, good things will happen. While this concept has its merits, relying solely on positive thinking can leave you feeling frustrated, stuck, and even more disconnected from your true self. It's not that positivity is bad—it's that it's incomplete.

Imagine you're going through a rough time. Maybe you've lost a job, ended a relationship, or are facing health challenges. Well-meaning friends might tell you to "stay positive" or "look on the bright side." On the surface, this advice seems encouraging, but deep down, it can feel dismissive. When you're in pain, trying to plaster over it with forced positivity doesn't heal the wound—it hides it. You're left grappling with the same feelings underneath, now compounded by guilt for not being able to "just think positive."

The problem with positivity on its own is that it ignores the complexity of human emotions. Life isn't always sunshine and rainbows and pretending it is doesn't make the storms go away. In fact, pushing away negative thoughts and feelings can often make them stronger.

Psychologists refer to this as the "white bear effect," where attempting to avoid thinking about something only makes it occupy your mind more. So, when you tell yourself to "just be positive," you might actually end up focusing even more on the very things you're trying to avoid.

True transformation doesn't come from ignoring the negative—it comes from learning how to face it with courage and compassion. This means acknowledging your difficult emotions instead of trying to suppress them. It means understanding that you can hold space for both positivity and pain at the same time. You can hope for a better future while also honoring the challenges of the present. This isn't about being optimistic or pessimistic; it's about being realistic.

Positive thinking also tends to place too much emphasis on the mind's ability to control outcomes. While your mindset is undeniably powerful, it's not the only factor that shapes your life. There are external circumstances, other people's actions, and random events that are beyond your control. When you believe that positive thinking alone will bring you success, you might feel like a failure when things don't go as planned. This isn't because you didn't "think hard enough"—it's because life is inherently unpredictable.

To truly break free from limiting beliefs and transform your life, you need more than just positive thinking—you need what I call *empowered thinking*. Empowered thinking is grounded in reality while still leaving room for hope and possibility.

It starts with accepting the present moment as it is, without trying to force it into something it's not. Instead of denying your pain or struggles, you face them head-on, knowing that they don't define you. At the same time, you allow yourself to dream, to take meaningful action, and to believe that change is possible.

Here's how to cultivate empowered thinking in your own life. First, when faced with a difficult situation, acknowledge it honestly. Instead of saying, "Everything's fine," try, "This is hard, and it's okay to feel this way." This simple act of self-validation can be incredibly freeing. Next, focus on what you can control. Reflect on this: "What is one small action I can take today to make progress?" This transforms your energy from merely hoping to actively participating.

Finally, practice gratitude—not as a way to ignore your struggles, but as a way to balance them. Gratitude helps you see the bigger picture, reminding you that even in challenging times, there are moments of beauty and connection to hold onto. It's not about forcing yourself to feel grateful for everything; it's about noticing the small, meaningful things that bring light into your life.

When you shift from positive thinking to empowered thinking, you create a mindset that's both hopeful and resilient. You stop blaming yourself when things don't go as planned and start seeing challenges as opportunities for growth. You become less attached to outcomes and more focused on the process of living fully, authentically, and courageously.

Next, we'll explore another common trap of the mind: the illusion of over-control. You'll learn why the need to micromanage every detail of your life often backfires and discover how letting go can lead to greater peace and freedom. For now, take a moment to reflect on the difference between positivity and empowerment. What would it feel like to embrace your full range of emotions without judgment, knowing that each one has something to teach you? Turn the page, and let's dive deeper into this journey of transformation.

The Illusion of Over-Control

The desire for control is deeply ingrained in us. It's part of being human. Control makes us feel safe, gives us a sense of order, and reassures us that we have power over our lives. But what happens when this natural desire turns into an illusion—when we convince ourselves that if we can just manage every detail, we'll be able to avoid pain, uncertainty, or failure? The truth is, the more we cling to control, the more it slips through our fingers.

The illusion of over-control begins with good intentions. You tell yourself that if you think about a situation enough, plan for every possible outcome, and micromanage every step, you'll achieve the perfect result. But life rarely unfolds according to plan. No amount of preparation can account for every variable, every surprise, every moment of randomness.

When you believe you can control everything, you set yourself up for frustration and disappointment when things inevitably veer off course.

Think about the last time you tried to control something beyond your reach. Maybe it was a conversation where you rehearsed every possible response, only to find the other person reacted in a way you couldn't anticipate. Or perhaps you meticulously planned an event, only to have an unforeseen hiccup throw everything off track. How did you feel in those moments? Most likely, you experienced a mix of anxiety, anger, and helplessness—the very feelings you were trying to avoid in the first place.

Over-control also keeps you trapped in a state of hypervigilance. When you believe it's your job to manage every outcome, your mind never gets a break. It's constantly scanning for problems, analyzing scenarios, and revisiting the past to identify what you could have done differently. This level of mental effort is exhausting, leaving you depleted and emotionally stretched thin. And even worse, it takes you out of the present moment, chaining you to an endless loop of what-ifs and should-haves.

At its core, over-control is driven by fear. Fear of failure, fear of uncertainty, fear of being vulnerable. But here's the irony: the harder you try to control everything, the more you reinforce those fears. Every time you try to take control and things don't go as planned, your mind says, "See? You didn't prepare well enough." You need to try harder next time." And so the cycle continues, keeping you locked in a perpetual battle against an unpredictable world.

Breaking free from the illusion of over-control doesn't mean giving up on responsibility or abandoning your goals. It means recognizing the limits of your influence and learning to focus on what you can control while letting go of what you can't. This isn't about resignation—it's about empowerment. When you stop trying to control the uncontrollable, you free up your energy to focus on what truly matters.

One way to practice letting go is to ask yourself: "What is within my control right now?" In any situation, there are always aspects you can influence and aspects you can't. You can control your actions, your mindset, and how you respond to challenges. But you can't control other people's reactions, random events, or the outcome of every effort. By shifting your focus to what's within your power, you reclaim your mental and emotional energy.

Another powerful strategy is to embrace uncertainty. This doesn't mean you have to like it—it simply means acknowledging that uncertainty is a natural part of life. Rather than perceiving it as a threat, consider it an opportunity to grow. When you let go of the need to predict every detail, you create space for spontaneity, creativity, and unexpected blessings.

Letting go also requires trust. Trust in yourself, trust in others, and trust in the process of life.

This doesn't mean blindly hoping for the best; it means believing that no matter what happens, you have the resilience to handle it. Trust allows you to release the need for control without feeling powerless.

Finally, practice self-compassion. When things don't go as planned, it's easy to blame yourself or feel like you've failed. But the truth is, life is messy and unpredictable for everyone. Instead of criticizing yourself, remind yourself that you're doing the best you can with the tools you have. Celebrate the effort you've put in, even if the outcome isn't what you hoped for.

The illusion of over-control isn't something you overcome in a single moment—it's a habit you unlearn over time. Each time you choose to let go, even a little, you loosen the grip of fear and create more room for peace and freedom. Life doesn't need to be an endless struggle for control. It can be an unfolding dance between intention and acceptance, effort and surrender.

In the next chapter, we'll explore what it means to reclaim your mental freedom. You'll learn practical tools to quiet the noise in your mind, break free from limiting patterns, and create space for clarity and creativity. Freedom begins when you let go of the need to hold on so tightly. Turn the page, and let's take the next step together.

Chapter 5: Reclaiming Your Mental Freedom

Mental freedom isn't about silencing your thoughts or erasing them entirely. It's about creating a new relationship with your mind—one where your thoughts don't control you, but instead, become tools you use with intention and purpose. Reclaiming your mental freedom is like stepping out of a cage you didn't realize you were in. It's the realization that your mind, for all its complexity and noise, is not your master. It's a companion you can train, guide, and ultimately make peace with.

The first step toward mental freedom is recognizing the difference between awareness and entanglement. Awareness is when you notice your thoughts without judgment or reaction. Entanglement, on the other hand, is when you get caught up in your thoughts, treating them as truths or instructions you must follow. For most of us, entanglement happens automatically. A thought appears, such as "I'm not good enough" or "What if I fail?"—and we immediately accept it as fact, letting it shape our emotions and actions. But when you cultivate awareness, you create a pause between your thoughts and your reactions. In that pause lies your freedom.

One of the most effective ways to build awareness is through mindfulness. Mindfulness is not about clearing your mind but about observing it.

Dedicate a few minutes daily to sit quietly with your thoughts. Close your eyes, take a deep breath, and let your mind roam freely. Rather than interacting with your thoughts, picture them as clouds floating across the sky. Some will be dark and heavy, others light and fleeting. Your job is to notice them without attaching to them. This practice trains you to see your thoughts for what they are: temporary, ever-changing, and often untrue.

Another powerful tool for reclaiming mental freedom is self-inquiry. This involves questioning the thoughts that cause you stress or suffering. When a limiting thought arises, ask yourself: "Is this true? Do I know for certain that it's true?" You'll often discover the answer is no. Then ask yourself: "What evidence supports this thought? What evidence goes against it?" This approach challenges the automatic acceptance of your thoughts and encourages fresh perspectives.

Let's consider an example. Imagine you're preparing for a big presentation, and the thought "I'm going to mess this up" keeps playing in your mind. Without awareness, this thought might trigger anxiety, self-doubt, and even avoidance. However, through self-inquiry, you take a moment to question the thought. Is it true that you'll mess up? Do you have proof that this will happen? Or is it just a fear-based assumption? You might realize that you've given successful presentations before or that even if you make a mistake, it won't define you. By questioning the thought, you take away its power.

Another aspect of mental freedom is learning to let go of control over things that aren't yours to control. This means accepting that you can't dictate how others feel, think, or act, and you can't predict every outcome. Instead of trying to control the uncontrollable, redirect your energy to what's within your power: your actions, your mindset, and your responses. This shift not only reduces stress but also empowers you to focus on what truly matters.

Cultivating gratitude is another pathway to mental freedom. Gratitude doesn't erase challenges or struggles, but it shifts your focus from what's lacking to what's present. Take a moment each day to think about three things you're thankful for. They don't have to be grand—sometimes it's the warmth of the sun on your face, a kind word from a friend, or even the breath in your lungs. Gratitude grounds you in the present and reminds you that, even in difficult times, there's light to be found.

As you reclaim your mental freedom, you may notice subtle changes. The thoughts that once felt overwhelming will lose their intensity. The situations that used to paralyze you with fear will feel more manageable. You'll find yourself reacting less and responding more, choosing your actions from a place of clarity rather than compulsion. This is the power of mental freedom: it doesn't eliminate life's challenges, but it changes how you experience and approach them.

Reclaiming your mental freedom isn't a one-time event; it's a lifelong practice.

Each time you choose awareness over entanglement, curiosity over judgment, and presence over control, you strengthen your ability to live with intention and peace. It's a journey of small, consistent steps, each one bringing you closer to the life you've always wanted to live.

Let us dive into practical strategies to break the cycle of overthinking and limiting beliefs. You'll learn actionable steps you can take right now to quiet your mind, shift your perspective, and move forward with confidence.

Practical Strategies to Break the Cycle

Breaking free from overthinking and reclaiming your mental freedom doesn't just happen by understanding the concept—it requires action. Practical strategies give you the tools to interrupt the mental loops that keep you stuck and redirect your energy toward clarity, confidence, and peace. These steps are not about perfection; they're about progress. Each one builds your ability to challenge old patterns and open the door to new possibilities.

Start with a simple but transformative habit: the mental pause. The next time you catch yourself spiraling into overthinking, stop and ask yourself, *What am I focusing on right now?* Often, overthinking thrives on projecting fears into the future or replaying mistakes from the past. By asking this question, you bring your attention back to the present.

Follow up with a grounding action: take three deep breaths, feel the sensations in your body, or focus on a physical object near you. This practice helps you interrupt the cycle and reconnect with the here and now.

Another strategy is to reframe your thoughts. Overthinking often comes from attaching negative meanings to situations or outcomes. For example, if you're stuck on a missed opportunity, you might be telling yourself, "This was my only chance, and I blew it." Reframing involves consciously shifting that perspective. Instead, you could think, "That wasn't the right opportunity for me, and now I have the chance to find one that's an even better fit." Reframing doesn't mean ignoring reality—it means choosing a perspective that empowers rather than diminishes you.

Journaling is another powerful tool to break the overthinking cycle. Set aside ten minutes each day to write down your thoughts without judgment or editing. Let everything pour out onto the page—the worries, the fears, the self-doubt. Once you've finished, take a moment to review what you've written. Ask yourself: *Are these thoughts facts, or are they assumptions? Do they reflect the reality of the situation, or are they driven by fear?* Journaling creates distance between you and your thoughts, making it easier to see them for what they are: stories, not truths.

Visualization can also help you shift out of overthinking. Close your eyes and picture a stop sign whenever you notice your thoughts starting to spiral.

This mental image serves as a reminder to pause and redirect your focus. From there, visualize a calm and peaceful scene—perhaps a quiet beach, a serene forest, or any place that brings you a sense of ease. Pair this visualization with slow, steady breaths, allowing your mind to settle. Visualization not only breaks the cycle of overthinking but also fosters a sense of inner calm.

One of the most effective strategies to break free from overthinking is setting boundaries with your mind. If you find yourself ruminating about a particular issue, allocate a specific "worry time" for it. For example, give yourself 15 minutes in the evening to think about the problem. During this time, write down your thoughts or brainstorm potential solutions. When the time is up, close the notebook or set aside the thoughts until the next scheduled session. This approach prevents overthinking from taking over your entire day and teaches your mind that not every worry needs your immediate attention.

Movement is another way to disrupt overthinking. When you're stuck in your head, shift your focus to your body. Go for a walk, do some stretching, or engage in a physical activity you enjoy. Movement not only relieves tension but also helps release the energy that overthinking tends to build up. It's a reminder that you are more than your thoughts—you are a whole, dynamic being with the power to choose action over rumination.

Lastly, practice gratitude as a daily ritual. Overthinking often stems from a focus on what's wrong or what could go wrong.

Gratitude shifts your attention to what's right. Write down three things you're grateful for each morning or evening. These can be small, like the warmth of a cup of coffee, or significant, like the support of a friend. Gratitude doesn't solve every problem, but it creates a mental environment where overthinking has less room to thrive.

As you integrate these strategies into your life, you'll notice subtle shifts. The mental spirals that once consumed you will start to loosen their grip. The decisions that felt overwhelming will become more manageable. And most importantly, you'll create space for clarity, creativity, and inner peace to flourish.

The Three-Step Process to Let Go of Overthinking

Letting go of overthinking isn't about silencing your thoughts or forcing your mind to "be still." It's about recognizing the patterns that trap you, challenging them with clarity, and shifting your focus to what serves you. This process isn't magic—it's a skill you can develop, and like any skill, it becomes easier with practice. The following three-step process will help you break free from overthinking and reclaim your peace, one thought at a time.

The first step is **Awareness**. You can't change what you don't notice. Overthinking thrives on autopilot, slipping into the background of your day until it feels like part of who you are.

To disrupt this cycle, you need to start paying attention to your thoughts. The next time you catch yourself spiraling, pause and ask: *What am I thinking about right now?* This simple question shifts your focus from being immersed in your thoughts to observing them. Imagine stepping outside yourself and watching your mind like a curious bystander. What patterns do you see? Are your thoughts repetitive? Do they focus on fear, regret, or worst-case scenarios?

Awareness also involves identifying the triggers that set off your overthinking. Is it a specific situation, like receiving an ambiguous email or making an important decision? Or is it a particular feeling, like uncertainty or fear of failure? By recognizing your triggers, you can anticipate them and prepare to respond differently. Awareness isn't about judging your thoughts—it's about shining a light on them so they no longer operate in the shadows.

The second step is **Disruption.** Once you're aware of your overthinking, the next step is to interrupt it. Overthinking feeds on momentum, so the sooner you disrupt the cycle, the easier it is to stop. A powerful way to do this is by asking, *Is this helpful?* Not all thoughts are worth your time and energy, and this question helps you determine which ones are. If your thoughts are focused on problem-solving or meaningful reflection, they may serve you. But if they're circling the same doubts or fears without progress, it's time to let them go.

One effective disruption technique is called *thought labeling.*

When a negative or unhelpful thought arises, label it for what it is: "That's fear," or "That's self-doubt." This simple act of naming your thought creates distance between you and it. Instead of being swept away, you can see it for what it is—a mental event, not a reflection of reality. Pair this labeling with a grounding action, like taking a deep breath or focusing on a physical sensation, to anchor yourself in the present moment.

The final step is **Redirection**. After disrupting your overthinking, it's essential to guide your mind toward something constructive. Without redirection, your thoughts are likely to fall back into old patterns. Start by asking yourself, *What can I focus on right now that's within my control?* Maybe it's taking one small step toward a goal, engaging in an activity that brings you joy, or simply being present with what's around you. Redirection isn't about ignoring your thoughts—it's about choosing to focus your energy on what matters most.

Visualization can be a powerful tool for redirection. Picture a box in your mind and imagine placing your overthinking thoughts inside it. Close the lid and set the box aside, knowing you can come back to it later if needed. Then, turn your attention to something positive or neutral—a calming memory, a task at hand, or the beauty of the present moment. By consciously shifting your focus, you reclaim your mental space and create room for peace.

This three-step process—awareness, disruption, and redirection—gives you a practical framework for managing overthinking in real time. It doesn't require perfection, and it's not about eliminating thoughts. Instead, it empowers you to respond to your mind with intention, breaking free from the automatic loops that once held you captive.

As you practice these steps, you'll start to notice a shift. The thoughts that once felt overwhelming will lose their intensity. The decisions that seemed impossible will feel more approachable. And the mental clarity you've been searching for will begin to emerge, one mindful choice at a time.

In the next chapter, we'll dive deeper into the root of many overthinking patterns: limiting beliefs. You'll learn how to recognize the beliefs that have been holding you back and discover practical strategies to replace them with empowering ones. For now, take a moment to reflect on the progress you've already made. Each step you take toward reclaiming your mental freedom is a step toward the life you truly deserve. Turn the page—the journey is just beginning.

Chapter 6: How to Recognize and Replace Limiting Beliefs

Limiting beliefs are the invisible chains that hold us back from realizing our potential. They often whisper doubts and fears, keeping us small and uncertain. The most dangerous part? They feel like the truth. These beliefs form in our minds, often without us even noticing, and quietly shape the way we think, feel, and act. Recognizing and replacing them is one of the most powerful steps you can take toward creating a life of freedom and authenticity.

To recognize a limiting belief, you first need to understand where it comes from. These beliefs usually develop early in life, shaped by your experiences, environment, and the messages you've absorbed from others. Maybe you were told as a child that "money doesn't grow on trees," and now you believe financial success is always out of reach. Or perhaps you failed at something important and concluded, "I'm just not good enough." Over time, these statements become part of your internal narrative, replaying in the background like a script you didn't write but have been acting out, nonetheless.

The tricky part is that limiting beliefs often hide in plain sight. They don't announce themselves as "beliefs"—they masquerade as facts.

You might think, "I'm too old to start something new," or "I could never do what they're doing," and not even question the validity of those thoughts. But these are not universal truths; they are interpretations, and interpretations can be changed.

To uncover your limiting beliefs, start by looking at the areas of your life where you feel stuck or dissatisfied. Reflect on your thoughts and ask, "What are my beliefs about this situation?" Then dig deeper: "Why do I believe that? Where did this belief come from? Is it true?" This type of self-reflection may feel uncomfortable initially, but it's crucial for letting go of outdated narratives that hold you back.

Once you've identified a limiting belief, the next step is to challenge it. One effective way to do this is by seeking evidence that contradicts the belief. For example, if your belief is "I always mess things up," look for moments in your life where you succeeded or handled a situation well. Write them down. This process helps you see that your belief is not a universal truth—it's a selective narrative your mind has been holding onto.

Another powerful technique is reframing. Reframing doesn't mean pretending everything is perfect; it means choosing a perspective that empowers you. Instead of "I'll never be good at this," try, "I'm learning and improving every day." Instead of "I'm too old," try, "I bring valuable life experience to this opportunity." Reframing isn't about lying to yourself—it's about focusing on possibilities rather than limitations.

Visualization can also be a helpful tool for replacing limiting beliefs. Close your eyes and imagine yourself living as though the limiting belief no longer exists. What would you do differently? How would you feel? Visualize yourself succeeding, thriving, and embracing challenges with confidence. This practice helps your mind create a new template for what's possible, rewiring old patterns over time.

The final and most crucial step is taking action. Beliefs are strengthened or weakened by the actions we take. If you believe you're not good enough and avoid opportunities because of it, that belief becomes reinforced. But if you take a small step outside your comfort zone—despite the belief—you begin to challenge its validity. Over time, these actions build evidence that the belief isn't true, allowing you to replace it with something more empowering.

For example, if you've always thought, "I'm not good at public speaking," begin with something small. Speak up in a meeting or practice a short speech in front of a trusted friend. Each action, no matter how small, chips away at the old belief and lays the foundation for a new one: "I'm capable of improving and growing."

Replacing limiting beliefs isn't about flipping a switch—it's about creating a new story for yourself, one step at a time. It's about choosing beliefs that align with the life you want to create, rather than the fears you've been taught to live by. And as you do, you'll find that the barriers you once thought were insurmountable were never real—they were just stories you no longer have to believe.

In the next section, we'll explore specific tools for challenging false assumptions. You'll learn practical exercises to question the stories your mind tells you and replace them with narratives that support your growth and freedom. For now, take a moment to consider the beliefs that have been shaping your life. What would change if you chose to see them differently?

Tools for Challenging False Assumptions

Breaking free from false assumptions is like clearing a fog from your mind. It's a process of gently but firmly questioning the stories you've been telling yourself and replacing them with truths that empower you. These assumptions often feel so embedded in our thinking that they seem like facts. But with the right tools, you can dismantle these mental roadblocks and rebuild a mindset that supports your growth and freedom.

One of the most powerful tools for challenging false assumptions is asking better questions. When you catch yourself thinking something like, "I'll never succeed at this," don't stop at the statement—interrogate it. Ask yourself, *Is this true?* Follow it up with, *What evidence do I have that supports this belief? What evidence contradicts it?* Often, you'll find that the evidence for your limiting assumption is flimsy or even nonexistent. By questioning your thoughts in this way, you shift from blindly accepting them to actively evaluating them.

Another question to ask is, *Where did this assumption come from?* Many of our limiting beliefs originate from childhood experiences, societal messages, or moments of vulnerability. For example, if you believe "I'm not creative," it might be because someone dismissed your ideas when you were younger. Recognizing the source of your assumption can help you see it for what it is: a reflection of a past moment, not an unchangeable truth about who you are.

Reframing is another essential tool for challenging false assumptions. Reframing doesn't deny your experiences—it helps you see them from a new perspective. If your mind tells you, "I always fail at everything," pause and reframe it: "I've faced challenges in the past, but I've also learned and grown from them." This shift in perspective doesn't erase the struggle, but it opens the door to possibility. It reminds you that your past doesn't dictate your future.

Journaling can be a powerful way to put these tools into practice. Take a limiting belief you've been holding onto and write it down at the top of a page. Then, underneath it, list all the evidence that supports the belief, followed by all the evidence that contradicts it. You might find that the supporting evidence is based on isolated incidents, while the contradictory evidence reveals a broader, more balanced truth. This exercise helps you separate fact from fear and gives you the clarity to move forward.

Visualization is another effective technique for dismantling false assumptions.

Close your eyes and picture yourself as the version of you who no longer believes the limiting thought. How do you stand? How do you speak? What choices do you make? Visualization helps your mind create a new narrative, one that aligns with your potential rather than your past doubts.

Another practical tool is creating an *evidence list*. This is a running list of times when you've succeeded, overcome challenges, or proven your limiting assumptions wrong. Whenever you doubt yourself, revisit this list. It's a tangible reminder of your capabilities and a counterbalance to the false stories your mind may try to tell you.

Finally, act, no matter how small. False assumptions lose their power when you prove them wrong through experience. If you believe, "I'm terrible at meeting new people," challenge that assumption by starting a conversation with someone. It doesn't have to be a grand gesture—even small actions build evidence that your assumption isn't true. Each step you take chips away at the false belief and replaces it with confidence.

Breaking free from false assumptions is a process, not an overnight transformation. It requires patience, practice, and compassion for yourself. There will be moments when the old beliefs resurface, but each time you challenge them, you weaken their grip. Over time, you'll find that the assumptions that once felt so solid are nothing more than shadows of doubt.

Take a moment to reflect on the tools you've explored. What limiting assumption are you ready to challenge today?

Turning Self-Doubt into Empowerment

Self-doubt can feel like a relentless critic in the back of your mind, questioning your every decision and reminding you of every perceived flaw. It whispers, "What if you fail? What if you're not enough? What if you don't deserve this?" For many people, this internal dialogue acts as an obstacle to growth, preventing them from achieving their full potential. But what if self-doubt wasn't your enemy? What if, instead of silencing it, you could transform it into a source of strength and empowerment?

The first step to turning self-doubt into empowerment is recognizing that doubt is not the problem—how you respond to it is. Doubt often arises when you're stepping into new or uncertain territory. It's your mind's way of trying to protect you from failure or rejection. While this intention is well-meaning, the execution is flawed. Instead of listening to self-doubt as a warning to stop, you can reframe it as a signal that you're on the verge of growth. Doubt shows up when you're pushing past your comfort zone, and that's exactly where transformation happens.

Start by acknowledging your self-doubt without judgment. Instead of thinking, "Why do I always doubt myself?" try, "I'm noticing doubt right now, and that's okay." This shift in perspective allows you to separate yourself from the emotion. You are not your doubt—you are the observer of it. This distinction is critical because it creates space for you to choose how to respond.

One effective way to reframe self-doubt is to treat it as curiosity rather than fear. When a doubtful thought arises, ask yourself, "What is this doubt trying to tell me?" Often, it's pointing to areas where you feel unprepared or unsure. Use this as an opportunity to gather more information, build your skills, or seek support. For example, if you're doubting your ability to succeed in a new job, identify specific areas where you'd like to grow and take actionable steps to address them. This proactive approach shifts your focus from what you can't do to what you can do.

Another powerful technique is to counteract self-doubt with evidence of your capabilities. Create a "confidence inventory" by listing accomplishments, strengths, and moments when you've overcome challenges in the past. Keep this list somewhere accessible, and revisit it whenever doubt creeps in. Seeing tangible proof of your resilience and success reminds you that you are capable of handling whatever comes your way.

Visualization can also help you transform doubt into empowerment.

Close your eyes and imagine the version of yourself who has already succeeded in the situation you're doubting. How does this version of you feel, think, and act? Visualize yourself stepping into that energy, embodying confidence and self-assurance. This practice helps bridge the gap between where you are and where you want to be, reinforcing that success is possible.

Self-compassion is another essential ingredient in this process. When doubt arises, it's easy to criticize yourself for not being confident enough or for feeling insecure. But berating yourself only amplifies the doubt. Instead, respond to yourself with kindness. Imagine what you would say to a close friend who was feeling the same way. Perhaps you'd remind them of their strengths, reassure them that it's okay to feel nervous, or encourage them to keep going despite the fear. Offer yourself the same grace and encouragement.

Acting, even in the smallest way, is perhaps the most transformative step in overcoming self-doubt. Doubt thrives in inaction because it has nothing to challenge it. But when you take a step forward, no matter how small, you create momentum. Each action provides evidence that your doubt is not a predictor of failure. For instance, if you're doubting your ability to write a book, start with one paragraph. If you're doubting your ability to run a marathon, start with a short jog. Progress, not perfection, is what weakens the hold of doubt.

It's also important to remember that doubt is a universal experience.

Even the most successful people in the world experience moments of insecurity. The difference is that they don't let doubt dictate their actions. They feel the fear and move forward anyway. You can do the same. Each time you choose to act in the face of doubt, you strengthen your confidence and resilience.

Transforming self-doubt into empowerment is not about eliminating doubt—it's about changing your relationship with it. Instead of seeing doubt as a stop sign, see it as a stepping stone. Instead of viewing it as a limitation, view it as an invitation to grow. You don't have to wait for the doubt to disappear to act. You simply have to move forward, one step at a time, trusting that you have everything you need to succeed.

In the next chapter, we'll explore the role of intuition in making everyday decisions. You'll learn how to distinguish between the voice of your intuition and the noise of overthinking and discover how trusting your inner wisdom can lead to clarity and confidence. For now, take a deep breath and remind yourself: doubt is not a barrier—it's a bridge to something greater.

Chapter 7: The Role of Intuition in Everyday Decisions

Intuition often feels like a quiet nudge, a soft inner knowing that doesn't demand attention but offers profound clarity. It's the sense that something is right—or not—without needing a detailed explanation. Yet, in a world that places such high value on logic and evidence, intuition is frequently overlooked, misunderstood, or dismissed entirely. The truth is, your intuition is one of the most powerful tools you possess for making decisions, especially when logic alone falls short or becomes entangled in overthinking.

At its core, intuition is your mind and body working together to process information in ways that are faster and deeper than conscious thought. It draws from your past experiences, learned patterns, and subconscious knowledge to offer insights that feel immediate and instinctive. The challenge is that many of us have learned to distrust this inner voice, favoring analysis and external validation instead. Reconnecting with your intuition requires a blend of awareness, trust, and practice.

One way to begin cultivating your intuition is to pay attention to how it speaks to you. For some, intuition feels like a physical sensation—a tightening in the stomach, a sudden calm, or a sense of lightness. For others, it's more emotional, like a spark of excitement or a wave of unease. Start noticing these subtle signals in your daily life.

When faced with a decision, pause and ask yourself: *How does this feel in my body? What is my initial gut reaction?* Often, your intuition speaks before your mind has a chance to overanalyze.

Another key to tapping into your intuition is creating space for stillness. Intuition thrives in moments of quiet, when the noise of daily life settles, and your inner wisdom has room to emerge. This doesn't mean you need to spend hours meditating—though meditation can help. It can be as simple as taking a few deep breaths, going for a walk without distractions, or spending time in nature. These quiet moments help you connect with the messages your intuition is sending.

To build trust in your intuition, start small. Use it for low-stakes decisions, like choosing what to eat for dinner or which book to read next. Notice how it feels to follow your gut and what the outcomes are. As you gain confidence, you can begin applying intuition to larger decisions, like career moves or relationships. Over time, you'll learn to distinguish between the voice of your intuition and the noise of fear, doubt, or overthinking.

A powerful way to strengthen your connection to intuition is through reflection. Think back to times in your life when you trusted your gut and it led to a positive outcome. Write down these moments as a reminder of your intuition's reliability. Then, consider times when you ignored your intuition and later wished you had listened. What stopped you from trusting it?

What would have been different if you had followed it? Reflecting allows you to identify patterns and strengthens your trust in your inner wisdom.

It's important to acknowledge that intuition doesn't always provide crystal-clear answers. Sometimes it offers a feeling, a direction, or a gentle push to explore further. That's okay. Intuition isn't about predicting the future—it's about guiding you toward choices that align with your values, goals, and authentic self. When you pair intuition with thoughtful action, you create a powerful combination for making decisions that truly serve you.

Reconnecting with your intuition involves releasing the need for approval from others. Society often teaches us to look outside ourselves for answers—to seek approval, follow trends, or rely on experts. While external input can be valuable, it's no substitute for the wisdom within you. Trusting your intuition requires courage—the courage to believe that you know what's best for you, even when others disagree or when logic can't explain why.

As you begin to rely more on your intuition, you may encounter moments of doubt. This is normal. Intuition doesn't guarantee a perfect outcome, and it's not immune to mistakes. But even when things don't go as planned, your intuition helps you make decisions that feel right in the moment, grounded in authenticity rather than fear or pressure. Over time, you'll find that these intuitive choices lead to a life that feels more aligned, meaningful, and fulfilling.

For now, take a moment to reflect: What would your life look like if you trusted your intuition just a little more?

Trusting Your Gut While Avoiding Bias

Trusting your intuition can feel like unlocking a superpower—an unshakable sense of knowing that guides you toward the right decisions. But intuition isn't infallible. It's influenced by your experiences, emotions, and subconscious biases, which can sometimes distort its message. Learning to trust your gut while avoiding these biases is essential if you want to rely on your intuition with confidence.

Bias often masquerades as intuition, whispering thoughts that feel instinctive but are rooted in fear, assumptions, or past conditioning. For instance, you might avoid pursuing a new job opportunity because your "intuition" tells you it's too risky. But is it really intuition, or is it the fear of failure disguising itself as inner wisdom? Distinguishing true intuition from bias requires self-awareness, reflection, and practice.

The first step is understanding how biases form. Your mind is constantly processing information, drawing conclusions based on patterns and past experiences. This is helpful in many situations—it allows you to act quickly and efficiently without overthinking every decision. But it also means your mind can make assumptions that aren't entirely accurate.

For example, if you've been hurt in a past relationship, you might automatically assume that vulnerability leads to pain. This assumption can show up as a gut feeling to avoid emotional closeness, even when the situation doesn't warrant it.

To trust your intuition while minimizing bias, start by pausing and questioning the source of your feelings. When your intuition speaks, ask yourself, *What is this based on?* If it's rooted in a clear sense of peace, clarity, or alignment, it's likely true intuition. If it's tinged with fear, doubt, or anxiety, it might be a bias or an emotional reaction. By taking a moment to reflect, you can separate the signal from the noise.

Another way to challenge bias is to consider alternative perspectives. When your gut tells you something, ask, *What might someone else think about this situation?* For example, if you're hesitant to take a leap of faith in your career, imagine what advice a trusted mentor or friend would give you. This helps you step outside your immediate reaction and see the situation from a broader, more balanced perspective.

It's also helpful to test your intuition through small experiments. If your gut is urging you to act in a certain way, take a low-stakes step in that direction and observe the outcome. Does the decision bring you closer to peace and alignment, or does it create more confusion? Over time, these small experiments build trust in your intuition while helping you refine your ability to discern true guidance from bias.

Self-compassion plays a crucial role in this process. It's natural to make mistakes as you learn to trust your intuition. Sometimes you'll misinterpret a signal or act on a bias without realizing it. Instead of berating yourself, use these moments as opportunities for growth. Reflect on what happened, identify what you can learn, and move forward with renewed clarity.

To further minimize bias, cultivate mindfulness. Mindfulness helps you stay present and aware of your thoughts and feelings, making it easier to notice when bias is creeping in. For example, if you feel an overwhelming sense of urgency about a decision, mindfulness allows you to pause and ask, *Am I reacting out of fear, or is this truly my intuition guiding me?* This awareness allows you to respond thoughtfully instead of reacting impulsively.

Finally, remember that intuition and logic are not enemies—they're allies. While intuition provides a sense of direction, logic helps you evaluate the practicalities of your decision. Use them together to create a balanced approach. For instance, if your intuition tells you to pursue a new opportunity, use logic to assess the steps you need to take and the potential risks involved. This partnership between intuition and reason ensures that your decisions are both inspired and grounded.

Trusting your gut is an art, not a science. It requires patience, practice, and a willingness to listen deeply to yourself. But as you refine this skill, you'll find that your intuition becomes a trusted ally, helping you make decisions that align with your values, goals, and authentic self.

You'll learn how to recognize when fear is disguising itself as intuition and how to uncover the deeper truths that guide you toward growth and freedom. For now, reflect on when your intuition has served you well, and consider how to begin tuning into it more clearly.

How to Differentiate Fear from Wisdom

Fear and wisdom both speak to us from deep within, but their voices are profoundly different. Fear often shouts, drowning out other thoughts with urgency and doubt. Wisdom, on the other hand, speaks softly—it's steady, calm, and unwavering. The challenge lies in learning to recognize which voice is guiding you, especially in moments of uncertainty.

Fear is rooted in survival. It evolved to keep you safe, to alert you to danger, and to prevent you from making risky choices. But in today's world, fear often misfires, triggering overreactions to situations that don't actually threaten your safety. It can make you doubt your abilities, avoid taking healthy risks, or cling to comfort zones that no longer serve you. Fear's voice is often frantic and repetitive, saying things like, *"What if you fail? What will people think? What if this doesn't work out?"* It focuses on worst-case scenarios and exaggerates every possible challenge.

Wisdom, by contrast, doesn't rely on fear tactics. It doesn't badger or berate you. Instead, it offers clarity.

Wisdom's voice might say, *"This choice aligns with your values,"* or *"This path feels right, even if it's uncertain."* It acknowledges challenges but doesn't inflate them. Wisdom trusts your ability to navigate difficulties and grow through experience.

One way to differentiate fear from wisdom is to notice how each one feels in your body. Fear often creates tension—a tightness in your chest, a knot in your stomach, or a sense of restlessness. Wisdom, however, feels expansive. Even if the decision it points to is challenging, there's a sense of inner peace or alignment that comes with it. Pay attention to these physical cues—they are powerful indicators of whether you're reacting out of fear or being guided by wisdom.

Another key difference lies in the language each voice uses. Fear speaks in absolutes: *"You can't," "You'll fail," "You're not ready."* It leaves no room for possibility or nuance. Wisdom, on the other hand, speaks in balanced terms: *"This might be hard, but you can handle it,"* or *"Take the next step and see where it leads."* Wisdom acknowledges uncertainty without being paralyzed by it. It encourages exploration, growth, and trust in your ability to adapt.

To further distinguish fear from wisdom, consider the outcomes each voice leads to. Fear often keeps you stuck—avoiding risks, delaying decisions, or staying in situations that no longer serve you. Wisdom, however, moves you forward. It helps you make choices that align with your values and long-term goals, even if those choices are uncomfortable in the short term.

Ask yourself, *"If I follow this voice, where will it lead me? Will it bring me closer to the life I want, or will it keep me in a cycle of avoidance?"*

Journaling can be a helpful tool in this process. When you're grappling with a decision, write down what each voice is saying. Label one column "Fear" and the other "Wisdom." Notice the tone, content, and energy of each perspective. This exercise not only clarifies which voice is speaking but also helps you practice identifying wisdom in future situations.

Another way to access wisdom is through mindfulness. When fear takes over, your mind races, focusing on all the things that could go wrong. Mindfulness helps you return to the present moment, where wisdom resides. Pause for a moment, take a few deep breaths, and ask yourself, "What feels true right now?" *What choice aligns with my deepest values?"* This practice helps you bypass fear's noise and tune into your inner guidance.

Trusting wisdom doesn't mean eliminating fear entirely—it means learning to coexist with it. Fear will always be a part of your journey, especially when you're stepping into new territory. But instead of letting it drive your decisions, you can acknowledge its presence and choose to act from a place of wisdom. You might think, "I recognize you, fear. I understand you're trying to keep me safe, but I choose to move forward, guided by what I know is right."

Each time you choose wisdom over fear, you strengthen your ability to trust yourself. You build a life that reflects your values, not your anxieties. You take steps, no matter how small, toward the future you desire. And along the way, you discover that wisdom is not something external or rare—it's been within you all along, waiting to be heard.

In the next chapter, we'll explore how to create a life beyond limits by reimagining success and happiness. You'll learn to define these concepts on your terms, breaking free from societal expectations and crafting a life that truly fulfills you. For now, reflect on the moments when wisdom has guided you, even in the face of fear. What choices are waiting for you to trust that inner knowing?

Chapter 8: Reimagining Success and Happiness

Success and happiness are concepts we're taught to chase from a young age. Society hands us a checklist: get good grades, secure a well-paying job, find a partner, buy a house, and achieve visible markers of status. Happiness, we're told, will naturally follow once these boxes are ticked. What if you achieve those milestones but still feel unfulfilled? Or when you realize the life you're pursuing isn't the one you truly want?

To create a life beyond limits, we must begin by redefining success and happiness on our own terms. This requires breaking free from external expectations and tuning into what truly matters to you. It's about moving away from societal scripts and embracing a version of fulfillment that feels authentic and aligned with your values.

The first step is understanding that success and happiness are not one-size-fits-all. What fulfills one person may feel empty to another. For some, success might mean climbing the corporate ladder, while for others, it's about having the freedom to explore creative passions. Happiness can come from the simple joy of being with loved ones or the excitement of chasing big dreams. It's not about right or wrong—it's about what feels right to you.

To reimagine success, ask yourself: *What does success mean to me?*

Consider how you would define it if there were no expectations from family, friends, or society. What would your life look like if you were free to pursue what truly lights you up? Write down your thoughts, and don't be afraid to dream boldly. This exercise helps you uncover the values and desires that are uniquely yours.

Once you have clarity on your vision, reflect on whether your current life aligns with it. Are you working toward goals that truly matter to you, or are you chasing someone else's idea of success? If there's a disconnect, it's not a failure—it's an opportunity to recalibrate. Identify one small change you can make to bring your life closer to your vision, whether it's setting aside time for a passion project, reevaluating your career path, or prioritizing self-care.

Reimagining happiness involves a similar process of introspection. Happiness is often thought of as a destination—a place you'll arrive at once you achieve enough, earn enough, or prove enough. But true happiness isn't a finish line; it's a way of being. It's found in the moments when you're present, connected, and aligned with your values.

Ask yourself: *What brings me joy?* Think about the activities, relationships, and experiences that make you feel alive. Are these things present in your daily life? If not, how can you create space for them? Happiness often comes from the simplest pleasures—a walk in nature, a heartfelt conversation, or the satisfaction of creating something meaningful.

Another important shift is to embrace happiness as a choice, not a condition. External circumstances may influence your mood, but your overall sense of fulfillment comes from within. Practice gratitude by focusing on what's good in your life right now. This doesn't mean ignoring challenges or pretending everything is perfect—it's about recognizing the beauty and blessings that coexist with the difficulties.

As you redefine success and happiness, you'll likely encounter resistance from both within and outside yourself. Old beliefs and societal pressures may whisper that you're being unrealistic, selfish, or naïve. But remember, living authentically is not about seeking approval—it's about honoring your truth. Each step you take toward alignment strengthens your confidence and clarity, making it easier to keep moving forward.

Reimagining success and happiness isn't about abandoning ambition or settling for less—it's about pursuing goals that truly fulfill you. It's about recognizing that life's greatest rewards come from living in harmony with who you are, not from trying to fit into a mold that was never meant for you.

You'll learn how to set intentions that align with your values, break free from outdated expectations, and create a life that feels meaningful and sustainable. For now, take a moment to reflect: If you could design your life with no limits, what would it look like? What would success and happiness mean to you?

Why Your Goals Need a Fresh Perspective

Goals are often framed as the roadmap to success and happiness. They're the milestones we believe will validate our efforts and define our worth. Yet, how often do we stop to ask ourselves: *Are these goals truly mine? Do they reflect who I am and what I want, or are they borrowed from someone else's idea of success?* Many of us are chasing goals that feel more like obligations than aspirations. It's no wonder that, even when we achieve them, the sense of fulfillment we expect remains elusive.

To break free from this cycle, your goals need a fresh perspective—one that aligns with your values, desires, and the life you want to create. Redefining your goals isn't about abandoning ambition; it's about ensuring that your ambition serves you, rather than the other way around.

The first step is to evaluate the origin of your goals. Reflect on why you set this goal initially. Is it rooted in genuine passion, or does it stem from societal pressure, fear of judgment, or the need for external validation? For example, if your goal is to climb the corporate ladder, consider whether it's driven by your love for the work or by the belief that higher status will make you more worthy. If your goal is to have a perfect home or an enviable lifestyle, ask if it's truly what you want or if it's an attempt to meet someone else's expectations.

Once you've identified the origins of your goals, the next step is to determine whether they still serve you.

Goals are not static—they should evolve as you grow and change. A goal that made sense five years ago may no longer resonate with who you are today. Allow yourself to release goals that no longer hold meaning for you. This isn't failure; it's growth. Releasing outdated goals creates space for new aspirations that reflect the person you're becoming.

Another critical aspect of giving your goals a fresh perspective is shifting from outcome-based goals to process-based goals. Outcome-based goals focus solely on the result: losing 20 pounds, earning a certain amount of money, or achieving a specific status. While these can be motivating, they often lead to frustration if the result takes longer than expected or doesn't deliver the satisfaction you hoped for. Process-based goals, on the other hand, emphasize the journey. Instead of focusing on losing 20 pounds, you might set a goal to move your body daily in ways that feel good. Instead of fixating on earning a certain amount, you might aim to consistently improve your skills and add value in your work. Process-based goals keep you engaged, fulfilled, and present in the moment, regardless of the outcome.

To create goals that feel fresh and aligned, consider using the "values first" approach. Start by identifying your core values—the principles that matter most to you, such as freedom, creativity, connection, or growth. Then, set goals that reflect those values. For example, if freedom is a core value, your goals might include building a flexible work schedule or creating financial independence.

If connection is a priority, you might focus on deepening relationships or contributing to your community. Goals rooted in your values are inherently meaningful because they reflect who you are at your core.

It's also important to prioritize intrinsic rewards over extrinsic ones. Intrinsic rewards are the joy, fulfillment, and growth you experience from the process itself, while extrinsic rewards are the external markers of success, like money, recognition, or status. When your goals are driven by intrinsic rewards, you're more likely to stay motivated and satisfied, even when challenges arise. For example, writing a book because you love the creative process is far more fulfilling than writing one solely to achieve bestseller status.

Finally, don't be afraid to dream big, but balance those dreams with actionable steps. A fresh perspective on goals means embracing both vision and practicality. Dreaming big inspires you, while taking small, consistent steps ensures progress. Divide your goals into smaller, achievable steps, and celebrate each milestone. Keep in mind that the journey holds as much value as the destination.

Reevaluating your goals can feel unsettling at first, especially if it involves letting go of long-held aspirations. But it's also liberating. It's an act of reclaiming your time, energy, and purpose. It's a declaration that your life is yours to shape, not a script to follow. Each new goal you set becomes a reflection of your true self, a step toward a life that feels deeply fulfilling and uniquely yours.

You'll discover practical ways to break free from societal expectations and find satisfaction in the choices and paths that resonate with your authentic self. For now, take a moment to reflect: If you could set goals without fear, judgment, or external pressure, what would they look like? Write them down.

Redefining Fulfillment on Your Terms

Fulfillment is often misunderstood. Many people see it as a distant destination, an endpoint they'll reach after accumulating enough achievements, wealth, or approval. Yet the truth is, fulfillment isn't something you find at the end of the road—it's something you cultivate along the way. It's deeply personal, shaped by your values, priorities, and the meaning you assign to your experiences. Redefining fulfillment on your terms means breaking free from societal scripts and creating a life that feels uniquely and authentically yours.

At its core, fulfillment is about alignment—living in harmony with your true self. It's the feeling you get when your actions reflect your values, when your choices are guided by what matters most to you, and when you give yourself permission to live a life that feels right, even if it doesn't look conventional. But redefining fulfillment requires courage because it means stepping away from what you've been told you "should" do and moving toward what you genuinely want.

The first step is to identify what fulfillment means to you. This might seem simple, but it's a process that requires honest reflection. Begin by reflecting on this question: *What brings me a sense of aliveness? What activities, relationships, or experiences bring me a sense of purpose and joy? What would I do if there were no expectations or judgments?* Write down your answers, even if they feel vague or uncertain at first. The goal is to uncover the threads of what truly matters to you.

Once you've identified these threads, look at your life as it is now. Are your daily choices and habits aligned with what you find fulfilling? If not, what small adjustments can you make to align them? Fulfillment doesn't require a complete overhaul of your life; often, it's about making subtle but intentional shifts. For example, if creativity is important to you, carve out time each week to write, paint, or explore other creative outlets. If connection is a core value, prioritize deepening relationships with people who uplift and inspire you.

Redefining fulfillment also means letting go of the belief that it's tied to perfection. Life will always have challenges, setbacks, and uncertainties, but these don't diminish your ability to feel fulfilled. Fulfillment often comes from how you navigate those challenges—by staying true to yourself, learning from the experience, and finding meaning even in difficult moments.

A meaningful way to achieve fulfillment is by concentrating on the present moment.

So much of life is spent chasing future goals or dwelling on past regrets that we miss the richness of what's happening right now. Practicing mindfulness helps you appreciate the small joys and victories that might otherwise go unnoticed—a kind word from a friend, the warmth of sunlight on your face, or the satisfaction of completing a meaningful task. These moments may seem insignificant, but together they form the foundation of a fulfilling life.

Another important aspect of fulfillment is gratitude. Gratitude shifts your perspective from what's missing to what's already present. Take a few minutes each day to reflect on what you're grateful for—whether it's the support of loved ones, growth opportunities, or simply the chance to begin again. Gratitude doesn't mean ignoring challenges; it means recognizing that even amid difficulty, there is something to appreciate.

As you redefine fulfillment, it's essential to release the idea that it looks the same for everyone. Your path is uniquely yours, and comparing it to others will only lead to frustration. Instead of measuring yourself against external benchmarks, focus on how your life feels to you. Are your actions aligned with your values? Are your decisions guiding you toward your true self? These are the questions that matter.

Finally, remember that fulfillment is not a static state—it's dynamic, evolving as you grow and change. The things that bring you joy and purpose today might look different a year from now, and that's okay.

Give yourself permission to reevaluate and adjust as needed. Fulfillment is less about reaching a fixed point and more about continually aligning with what feels true and meaningful.

Living a fulfilled life is not about doing more—it's about being more. Being more present. Being more authentic. Being more intentional. When you stop chasing fulfillment and start creating it, you'll find that it's not something "out there" to achieve. You can experience it here and now.

In the next chapter, we'll explore how to build emotional resilience—a skill that helps you navigate life's inevitable ups and downs while staying grounded in your sense of self. You'll discover practical strategies for bouncing back from setbacks, managing stress, and maintaining inner peace, even in challenging times. For now, take a deep breath and reflect: What would your life look like if fulfillment wasn't something you searched for but something you created every day? Turn the page, and let's continue shaping a life that feels whole and authentic.

Chapter 9: Building Emotional Resilience

Life presents us with moments that challenge our resilience. Whether it's an unexpected setback, a relationship challenge, or the internal battle of self-doubt and fear, emotional resilience is the key to not only surviving but thriving through it all. Resilience isn't about avoiding pain or difficulty—it's about building the inner strength to bounce back, learn, and grow from life's inevitable challenges. It's about creating a foundation of emotional stability that allows you to face the storm without being swept away.

Emotional resilience begins with acceptance. Often, we resist difficult emotions, wishing them away or pretending they don't exist. But suppressing pain doesn't make it disappear; it just drives it deeper, where it festers and grows. True resilience comes from allowing yourself to feel, without judgment or resistance. Acceptance doesn't mean you have to like what's happening—it simply means acknowledging your emotions and giving yourself permission to experience them. When you say to yourself, *"It's okay to feel this way,"* you take the first step toward processing and releasing those feelings.

Resilience also requires self-awareness. Emotional challenges often stem from the stories we tell ourselves about what's happening. For example, if you lose a job, you might tell yourself, *"I'm a failure. I'll never find something better."* These stories amplify the pain and make it harder to recover. Building resilience means questioning these narratives.

Ask yourself, *"Is this story true? Is it helpful? What else might be true?"* Shifting your perspective can turn a setback into a chance for growth.

Another powerful tool for resilience is self-compassion. When things go wrong, it's easy to turn on yourself, blaming and criticizing every misstep. However, self-criticism intensifies the pain, making recovery more difficult. Self-compassion, on the other hand, provides the emotional support you need to move forward. Talk to yourself the way you would to a close friend: "Mistakes are okay. You're doing your best, and you'll find a way through this." Self-compassion doesn't erase the pain, but it eases it, opening the door for healing to start.

Resilience also thrives on perspective. When you're in the middle of a tough situation, it can feel all-encompassing, as if the pain will never end. But every challenge is temporary, even if it doesn't feel that way in the moment. Remind yourself of past difficulties you've overcome and how you've grown from them. This perspective helps you see the current challenge as part of a larger journey—one that's shaping you into a stronger, wiser version of yourself.

Practical steps also play a crucial role in resilience. One of the most effective is building a support system. Resilience doesn't mean handling everything on your own—it's about knowing when to reach out for help.

Whether it's talking to a trusted friend, seeking guidance from a mentor, or working with a therapist, leaning on others can provide the perspective, encouragement, and strength you need to keep going. Connection is a powerful antidote to emotional overwhelm.

Another practical strategy is to focus on what you can control. Challenges often feel overwhelming because we fixate on the aspects we can't change. Resilience comes from shifting your attention to the things you *can* influence. When dealing with a tough situation, consider asking yourself, *"What small step can I take to make this better? What's within my power to change?"* Even the smallest actions—like making a plan, setting a boundary, or practicing self-care—can create a sense of agency and momentum.

Resilience also grows through intentional habits that support your emotional well-being. Regular exercise, sufficient sleep, healthy eating, and mindfulness practices create a foundation of stability that makes it easier to handle life's ups and downs. These habits don't eliminate challenges, but they give you the energy and clarity to face them with strength and grace.

Ultimately, emotional resilience is about trust—trust in yourself, trust in the process of growth, and trust in life's ability to surprise you with moments of joy and possibility, even after difficulty. Resilience is not a trait you're born with; it's a skill you develop through practice. Each time you face a challenge and choose to rise, you strengthen your capacity to handle whatever comes next.

As we continue, we'll delve deeper into the art of letting go—of anxiety, of self-doubt, and of the fears that keep you trapped in a cycle of emotional suffering. For now, reflect on this: What would your life look like if you believed in your ability to recover and grow from any challenge? That strength is already within you, waiting to be tapped. Let's uncover it together.

Letting Go of Anxiety and Self-Doubt

Anxiety and self-doubt are like uninvited guests in your mind, constantly whispering that you're not enough, that things will fall apart, or that you're doomed to fail. They thrive on uncertainty and feed on your deepest insecurities. But what if you could let them go—not by fighting against them, but by understanding and releasing the grip they hold over you? The truth is, anxiety and self-doubt don't define you. They are fleeting states, not permanent fixtures, and with the right approach, you can loosen their hold and create space for confidence, calm, and clarity.

The first step to letting go of anxiety is to understand its root. Anxiety often arises from a need for control—the desire to predict and prepare for every possible outcome. But life is inherently unpredictable, and the pursuit of control is exhausting and futile. Instead of trying to eliminate uncertainty, the key is to shift your relationship with it. Anxiety loses its power when you accept that you don't need all the answers right now.

Begin by reassuring yourself, *"It's okay not to have all the answers. I can handle what comes."* This simple shift can help you approach the unknown with curiosity rather than fear.

Self-doubt, on the other hand, thrives on comparison and unrealistic expectations. It convinces you that everyone else has it figured out, while you're somehow falling short. But self-doubt is a liar, and the best way to silence it is to challenge its assumptions. When self-doubt tells you, *"You're not good enough,"* ask yourself, *"According to whom? What evidence supports this? What advice would I give to a friend if they were in my situation?"* By questioning the stories self-doubt feeds you, you begin to see them for what they are: baseless fears, not facts.

Another powerful tool for letting go of anxiety and self-doubt is mindfulness. Anxiety often pulls you into the future, while self-doubt drags you into the past. Mindfulness anchors you in the present, where these emotions have less sway. When you notice anxious or doubtful thoughts creeping in, pause and take a deep breath. Focus on the sensations of the moment—the rhythm of your breath, the feel of the ground beneath your feet, or the sounds around you. This practice reminds you that the present is manageable, even if the past or future feels overwhelming.

It's also important to recognize that anxiety and self-doubt are not enemies to be defeated; they are signals from your mind. Anxiety may be trying to protect you from perceived danger, while self-doubt might be urging you to grow or reassess your approach.

Instead of resisting these emotions, listen to them with compassion. Ask yourself, *"What message is this feeling trying to convey? Is there a lesson here, or is this fear based on outdated beliefs?"* When you approach these emotions with curiosity rather than judgment, you gain valuable insights that help you move forward.

Letting go also involves self-compassion. Too often, we're harsh on ourselves for feeling anxious or doubtful, as if these emotions are weaknesses. But they are a natural part of being human, especially in a world that values perfection and certainty. Be as kind to yourself as you would be to a friend. When anxiety or self-doubt arises, say to yourself, *"It's okay to feel this way. I'm doing the best I can, and that's all that matters."* This small act of self-kindness creates a sense of security and calm, helping to dissolve fear.

Action is another antidote to both anxiety and self-doubt. These emotions thrive in stagnation, when your mind has time to ruminate and catastrophize. Taking even the smallest step toward your goals disrupts this cycle. If you're anxious about a presentation, practice your opening lines. If you're doubting your ability to start a new project, take one small action—research a topic, draft an outline, or set a timer for ten minutes of focused effort. Each step you take builds momentum and quiets the voice of doubt.

Finally, surround yourself with reminders of your resilience. Keep a journal of past challenges you've overcome, kind words from friends or mentors, or accomplishments that make you proud.

When anxiety and self-doubt strike, revisit these reminders to ground yourself in the truth: you are capable, resourceful, and stronger than you realize.

Letting go of anxiety and self-doubt doesn't mean you'll never feel them again. It means they'll no longer dictate your decisions or limit your potential. They may still visit, but they'll come as fleeting clouds, not permanent storms. And each time you face them with courage, you'll reinforce your ability to move through them with grace.

You'll learn practical strategies for embracing the unknown, trusting yourself, and finding stability even when everything feels uncertain. For now, take a moment to reflect: *What would you do if anxiety and self-doubt no longer held you back?* The possibilities are endless, and the tools to unlock them are waiting for you in the next chapter.

How to Navigate Life's Uncertainty with Grace

Uncertainty is an inevitable part of life. No matter how carefully you plan or how much control you try to exert, there will always be moments when the path ahead is unclear. While uncertainty can feel unsettling, it also holds the potential for growth, discovery, and transformation. The key lies in learning how to navigate it with grace—not by avoiding it or forcing clarity, but by embracing the unknown as an opportunity to deepen your resilience and trust in yourself.

The first step to navigating uncertainty is to acknowledge and accept it. Resistance only intensifies the discomfort, creating a mental tug-of-war between what you want and what is. Acceptance doesn't mean you have to like uncertainty; it simply means recognizing that it's a natural part of life. Remind yourself, *"It's okay not to have all the answers right now. I can still move forward."* This mindset shift turns uncertainty from an enemy into a neutral presence—something you can coexist with, rather than fear.

Perspective is a powerful ally in uncertain times. When faced with the unknown, it's easy to focus on worst-case scenarios, letting your imagination spiral into fear. But uncertainty is just as likely to bring positive outcomes as negative ones. Think of moments in your past when uncertainty led to unexpected blessings—a chance encounter that became a cherished friendship, a career shift that opened new doors, or a challenge that revealed your inner strength. Trusting that uncertainty holds potential as well as risk helps you approach it with curiosity rather than dread.

Another way to navigate uncertainty is to focus on what's within your control. Even when the big picture feels unclear, there are always small steps you can take to create stability. Break down your situation into manageable pieces and identify one action you can take today, no matter how small.

Whether it's organizing your thoughts, seeking advice, or simply taking a deep breath, each action reinforces your sense of agency.

Uncertainty becomes less overwhelming when you realize you can still influence your experience.

Embracing uncertainty also means being present in the moment. Anxiety about the future often pulls your attention away from the here and now, robbing you of the opportunity to find peace in what is. Practice grounding yourself by tuning into your senses. Pay attention to what you see, hear, and feel. Focus on your breath, letting its steady rhythm anchor you. By staying present, you remind yourself that while the future may be uncertain, this moment is manageable—and often more peaceful than your mind would have you believe.

Self-compassion is essential when navigating uncertainty. It's natural to feel vulnerable or unsure in the face of the unknown, but these feelings don't mean you're weak or incapable. Be kind to yourself. Remind yourself, "I'm doing my best, and I'll figure this out." Self-compassion will help you stay calm and focused, even when things are uncertain.

Flexibility is another crucial skill. Uncertainty often requires adapting to changing circumstances, letting go of rigid expectations, and staying open to new possibilities. Rather than clinging to a specific outcome, approach the situation with a mindset of exploration: *"What can I learn from this? What opportunities might this bring?"* Being flexible enables you to adapt to circumstances, transforming challenges into opportunities.

Building trust in yourself is perhaps the most transformative way to navigate uncertainty. Remind yourself of the challenges you've faced and overcome in the past. Each time you stepped into the unknown and emerged stronger, you proved your ability to handle life's unpredictability. Trusting yourself doesn't mean you'll always have the answers—it means believing in your capacity to learn, adapt, and grow, no matter what comes your way.

Lastly, remember that uncertainty is temporary. The fog will clear, the answers will come, and the path will reveal itself in time. Patience is an act of self-care in uncertain moments. While waiting for clarity, focus on nurturing yourself—emotionally, mentally, and physically. This creates a foundation of strength that will support you when the next steps become clear.

As you navigate uncertainty, keep this in mind: life's most meaningful transformations often begin in the unknown. The discomfort of not knowing is the seedbed of growth, creativity, and resilience. Each time you face uncertainty with grace, you strengthen your ability to thrive in a world that is ever-changing. Instead of fearing the unknown, you learn to embrace it as a vital part of the journey.

In the next chapter, we'll explore how to move from fear to freedom. You'll discover actionable steps to release fear's grip and reclaim your power, allowing you to step into a life defined not by limitations, but by endless possibilities.

For now, take a deep breath and consider this: *What if uncertainty isn't something to survive, but something to embrace? What lesson is it trying to impart??* Let's continue the journey together, turning the page toward a life of freedom and fulfillment.

Chapter 10: From Fear to Freedom

Fear can feel like a wall—immovable, impenetrable, and all-consuming. It paralyzes decision-making, clouds judgment, and keeps you trapped in a cycle of hesitation and avoidance. But fear isn't as solid as it seems. It's more like a shadow, taking on intimidating shapes in the absence of light. The journey from fear to freedom is about shining a light on these shadows, understanding their true nature, and stepping through them with courage and clarity.

The first step to moving beyond fear is recognizing that it is a natural, universal experience. Fear is hardwired into us as a survival mechanism, designed to protect us from danger. But in the modern world, fear often overreaches its original purpose. It convinces you that rejection, failure, or uncertainty are threats to your very existence, when in reality, they're simply part of being human. By understanding that fear is a signal, not a sentence, you can start to view it as a messenger rather than an obstacle.

To break free from fear, it's important to confront it directly. Fear grows in the dark, thriving on avoidance and uncertainty. When you avoid what you fear, you reinforce its power, allowing it to dictate your choices and limit your potential. Instead, approach fear with curiosity. Challenge your fears by asking yourself: 'What am I truly afraid of? What's the worst-case scenario, and how could I overcome it?'

Often, you'll discover that the reality of your fears is less daunting than your imagination.

Another key to overcoming fear is reframing it as an opportunity for growth. Fear often points to areas where you're stepping outside your comfort zone—areas ripe for learning and transformation. View fear as a guidepost, not a stop sign. It's an indication that you're venturing into new territory, stretching beyond the limits of who you've been. This perspective doesn't eliminate fear, but it shifts your relationship with it, allowing you to move forward even when fear is present.

One of the most effective ways to dissolve fear is through action. Fear feeds on inaction, amplifying your doubts and creating a loop of paralysis. But when you take even the smallest step toward what you fear, you begin to weaken its grip. Action is the catalyst for momentum, which fuels confidence. If you're afraid of speaking up, start by sharing your thoughts with a trusted friend. If you're afraid of failure, take one small risk that feels manageable. Each step you take sends a powerful message to your mind: *"I am capable. I can handle this."*

Self-compassion is also essential in the journey from fear to freedom. Fear often brings with it harsh self-criticism, a voice that says, *"You're weak for feeling this way. You'll never overcome this."* But beating yourself up only strengthens fear's hold. Instead, offer yourself kindness and understanding. Remind yourself that fear is part of being human, and it doesn't diminish your worth or strength.

Speak to yourself as you would to a friend facing the same fears: *"It's okay to feel scared. You're doing something brave, and that takes courage."*

Visualization is a potent tool for conquering fear. Close your eyes and imagine yourself on the other side of the fear, having accomplished what you set out to do. Picture the sense of relief, pride, and empowerment that comes from moving through the fear rather than letting it hold you back. This mental rehearsal not only calms your nervous system but also reinforces your belief in your ability to succeed.

Finally, remind yourself of your past victories over fear. Think of times when you faced something daunting and came out stronger on the other side. These experiences are proof of your resilience and capability. Each time you've faced fear before, you've grown—not just in confidence, but in your understanding of what you're truly capable of. Let these memories serve as fuel for the challenges ahead.

Freedom from fear doesn't mean never feeling it again. It means no longer allowing it to control your choices or define your life. It's about learning to coexist with fear, to hear its message without obeying it. Fear may whisper, *"What if you fail?"* but freedom responds, *"What if I succeed?"* Your courage, not fear, defines you with each step forward.

As we move forward, we'll explore how challenges—those moments of fear, uncertainty, and struggle—can be transformed into opportunities for personal growth.

The section chapter will guide you in using life's obstacles as stepping stones toward greater strength, wisdom, and fulfillment. For now, take a moment to reflect: *What fear have you been allowing to hold you back, and what small step can you take today to move through it?* The solutions you seek lie deep within you, waiting to be discovered. Let's embark on this journey together, taking each courageous step one at a time.

Using Challenges to Unlock Personal Growth

Challenges are the gateway to growth, though they rarely feel that way in the moment. When life throws obstacles in your path, it's easy to view them as barriers—reasons to turn back or question your abilities. But what if every challenge was an invitation to become more of who you are meant to be? What if each setback was a signpost pointing you toward greater strength, resilience, and clarity? Challenges don't exist to break you; they exist to shape you. They offer the raw material for transformation, waiting to be unlocked through your perspective and actions.

The key to using challenges for personal growth lies in how you interpret them. Too often, people see difficulties as proof of their inadequacy or as punishment for past choices. This mindset creates resistance, trapping you in frustration or despair. Instead, try reframing challenges as opportunities. Ask yourself, *"What can I take away from this? How is this experience helping me grow?"*

Shifting your perspective doesn't erase the difficulty, but it opens the door to growth by turning pain into purpose.

One of the most profound truths about challenges is that they reveal your hidden strengths. You don't know your limits until you push them. When you're forced to adapt, to rise to the occasion, you discover parts of yourself that you didn't know existed. The strength to endure, the courage to keep going, and the wisdom to find solutions—all of these emerge in the crucible of challenge. Think back to a time in your life when you overcame something you once thought impossible. That strength is still within you, waiting to be called upon again.

Challenges also force you to confront and release limiting beliefs. When life doesn't go as planned, it often exposes the stories you've been telling yourself—stories about what you can and cannot do, about what success should look like, or about what you think you deserve. These beliefs may have gone unnoticed in easier times, but challenges bring them to the surface. Use this as an opportunity to question them. Ask yourself, *"Is this belief helping me? Is it even true?"* To allow a new, more empowering narrative to emerge, we must first abandon these obsolete stories.

Another powerful way to unlock growth through challenges is to embrace vulnerability. Our culture often glorifies toughness, encouraging us to push through difficulties without showing weakness.

But vulnerability is not weakness; it's the foundation of authentic strength. When you allow yourself to feel your emotions fully—whether that's fear, sadness, or frustration—you release their hold on you. Vulnerability also opens the door to connection, allowing you to seek support and perspective from others. Sometimes, the greatest growth comes not from facing a challenge alone, but from learning to ask for and receive help.

Action is a crucial component of growth through challenges. It's easy to get stuck in analysis or overwhelm, wondering how to move forward. But growth doesn't require perfect steps—it just requires movement. Start small. Take one action, no matter how minor, toward addressing the challenge. Each step builds momentum and gives you a sense of agency, reminding you that you are not powerless. Even in the face of uncertainty, action creates clarity and opens new possibilities.

Reflection is equally important. After you've moved through a challenge, take time to look back and consider what it taught you. What did you learn about yourself? What skills or strengths did you develop? How might this experience prepare you for future obstacles? Reflection not only reinforces your growth but also helps you see challenges as meaningful parts of your journey rather than random disruptions.

Gratitude is a transformative mindset when facing challenges.

It may feel counterintuitive to be grateful for something difficult, but gratitude shifts your focus from what's wrong to what's possible. Even in the hardest moments, there are things to appreciate—the support of a friend, the lessons learned, or the resilience you're building. Gratitude doesn't minimize the difficulty, but it reframes it as part of a larger picture, one that includes both struggle and growth.

As you embrace challenges, remember that growth is not linear. Some days, you'll feel like you're making progress; other days, you may feel stuck or overwhelmed. This is normal. Growth is a process, not a destination. Trust that even when it feels like nothing is changing, the effort you're putting in is planting seeds that will bloom in time.

When you stop seeing challenges as barriers and start viewing them as stepping stones, you unlock a sense of freedom. No longer held back by fear of failure or discomfort, you begin to see each obstacle as a chance to evolve. This shift transforms your relationship with life itself, allowing you to meet its ups and downs with confidence and grace.

Next, we'll explore how to face life's unknowns with confidence, equipping you with practical tools to handle uncertainty while staying grounded in your own strength. For now, consider this: *What challenge in your life might be offering you the opportunity to grow? What would happen if you approached it with curiosity instead of fear?* The answers may surprise you—and they may just set you free.

How to Face Life's Unknowns with Confidence

Life's unknowns can feel like walking into a room with the lights off. You don't know where the edges are, where the obstacles might be, or how far you have to go before you'll find the switch. This uncertainty can be paralyzing, leaving you stuck in the doorway, too afraid to move forward. But what if you could step into that room with confidence, trusting that you have the tools to navigate whatever lies ahead? Facing the unknown is not about eliminating fear—it's about learning to act in spite of it, armed with a sense of inner stability that no external uncertainty can shake.

The first step to facing the unknown is grounding yourself in the present. When confronted with uncertainty, your mind often spirals into worst-case scenarios, pulling you out of the now and into an imagined future filled with "what-ifs." To combat this, concentrate on what you can influence now. Anchor yourself in what you know for sure—your values, your strengths, and the immediate actions you can take. This grounding helps you approach uncertainty not as an overwhelming force but as a series of moments you can handle, one step at a time.

Trust in your own resilience is another key to navigating the unknown with confidence. Often, fear of the unknown isn't about the situation itself but about doubting your ability to handle it.

But think of the challenges you've already overcome in lifetimes when you didn't know how things would turn out, yet you found a way through. Each of those experiences is evidence of your strength and adaptability. Remind yourself, *"I've faced uncertainty before, and I can do it again."* This mindset transforms the unknown from a threat into an opportunity to prove to yourself just how capable you are.

It's also important to release the need for perfection. Facing the unknown with confidence doesn't mean you'll always make the "right" decision or have everything figured out. It means giving yourself permission to learn as you go, to adjust your course when needed, and to accept that mistakes are part of growth. When you let go of the pressure to get it all right, you free yourself to take risks and move forward, even in the face of uncertainty.

Another powerful tool is reframing uncertainty as a possibility. While the unknown can feel like a void, it's also a blank canvas—an opportunity for something new and unexpected to emerge. Consider the potential exciting opportunities that this uncertainty may offer. *'What could I gain by stepping into the unknown?'* Shifting your focus from fear to curiosity opens your mind to creative solutions and allows you to approach uncertainty with a sense of adventure rather than dread.

Mindfulness is your ally in uncertain times. When your mind starts to spiral into anxiety about the future, mindfulness helps you return to the present moment, where the unknown hasn't yet materialized into anything concrete.

Practice deep breathing, focus on the sensations in your body, or simply observe your thoughts without judgment. This not only calms your nervous system but also creates space for clarity and intentional action.

Seeking support is another important step. You don't have to face life's unknowns alone. Whether it's a trusted friend, a mentor, or a community of like-minded individuals, having someone to share your thoughts with can provide perspective and reassurance. Often, simply voicing your fears helps to reduce their intensity and allows you to see the situation more clearly.

Action is the antidote to fear of the unknown. Even if you don't have all the answers, taking small, intentional steps helps you build momentum and confidence. Each action, no matter how minor, is a vote of trust in yourself and your ability to navigate uncertainty. Start with what you know and let the path unfold from there. Remember, clarity often comes from action, not the other way around.

Gratitude is a surprising but effective tool for facing the unknown. When uncertainty feels overwhelming, pausing to acknowledge what you're grateful for shifts your focus from what's missing to what's present. Gratitude doesn't solve the uncertainty, but it helps you approach it from a place of abundance rather than lack, reinforcing your sense of inner stability.

Finally, remind yourself that life itself is uncertain. Even the most carefully laid plans can change in an instant, and that's what makes life dynamic and full of potential. Embracing this truth allows you to stop resisting uncertainty and start living fully in the face of it. The unknown isn't something to fear—it's where growth, discovery, and transformation happen.

As you take these steps, notice how your relationship with uncertainty begins to shift. It's no longer a dark room filled with imagined dangers but a space of infinite possibility. With each step you take, you build not only your confidence but also your capacity to face whatever life may bring. You're not just surviving the unknown—you're thriving in it.

In the next chapter, we'll explore daily practices that help anchor your mind and enhance your clarity, no matter what challenges or uncertainties you face. These tools will empower you to move through life with greater ease and intention, transforming your everyday routines into a foundation for mental and emotional freedom. For now, take a moment to reflect: *What small action can you take today to step into the unknown with confidence?* The possibilities are waiting, and so is the next chapter of your transformation.

Chapter 11: Daily Practices for Mental Clarity

Mental clarity is not something you stumble upon by chance; it's a state you cultivate intentionally, a practice woven into the fabric of your daily life. It is the ability to see through the noise of your mind, to separate the essential from the extraneous, and to approach life with a calm and focused presence. In a world that thrives on distraction, clarity is a rare and invaluable gift—a gift you can give yourself through consistent, purposeful practices.

Clarity begins with creating space in your mind, and one of the most effective ways to do this is through mindful stillness. Start each day with a moment of quiet reflection, free from the pull of notifications and to-do lists. Whether it's sitting in silence, meditating, or simply focusing on your breath, this practice allows your mind to reset before the demands of the day take over. It's not about achieving a perfect state of Zen; it's about giving yourself permission to pause and reconnect with the present moment.

Another key practice for mental clarity is simplifying your surroundings. The clutter in your physical environment often mirrors the clutter in your mind. Take a few minutes each day to tidy up your space—clear your desk, organize a corner of your home, or sort through your belongings.

This small act of orderliness sends a powerful message to your brain: *You are in control. You are creating space for focus and clarity.*

Your body plays an integral role in your mental state, and nurturing it is a daily practice for clarity. Hydration, nutrition, and movement are not just physical necessities; they are foundational to a clear and focused mind. Begin your day with a glass of water, fuel yourself with foods that sustain your energy, and incorporate movement—whether it's a short walk, stretching, or a workout that invigorates you. These simple acts ground you in the present and energize your mind for what lies ahead.

Intentional breaks are another cornerstone of mental clarity. Productivity culture often glorifies constant busyness, but your brain needs moments of rest to function optimally. Schedule short breaks throughout your day to step away from your work, breathe deeply, and reset. These pauses are not indulgent; they are essential. They allow you to return to your tasks with renewed focus and creativity.

Practicing gratitude is a transformative habit for mental clarity. End each day by listing three things you're grateful for. This simple act shifts your focus from what's wrong or overwhelming to what is meaningful and positive. Gratitude rewires your brain to recognize abundance rather than scarcity, calming your mind and sharpening your perspective.

Setting boundaries is equally important. Mental clarity thrives in an environment where distractions are minimized and your time is respected. Create boundaries around your work, relationships, and personal time. This might mean turning off notifications during focused work hours, saying no to commitments that drain your energy, or dedicating time solely for yourself. Boundaries are not barriers; they are acts of self-respect that protect your mental space.

Reflection at the close of each day enhances clarity for the days ahead. Take a few minutes to review your day—what went well, what challenged you, and what you learned. This practice helps you process your experiences, learn from them, and carry that wisdom forward. It turns your daily life into a continuous cycle of growth and understanding.

Clarity also comes from alignment—ensuring your actions reflect your values and priorities. Begin each week by identifying one or two things that matter most to you and focus your energy on those. This intentionality helps you avoid getting swept up in distractions and keeps your mind clear and directed.

Mental clarity is not about achieving perfection. It's about showing up each day with intention, practicing habits that support your well-being, and giving yourself grace in the moments when your mind feels anything but clear. Over time, these practices create a foundation of calm, focus, and resilience that carries you through life's challenges with greater ease.

As you adopt these practices, you'll experience a shift in both your thoughts and feelings. Clarity becomes not just a fleeting experience but a way of being, a state you can return to whenever life feels overwhelming.

Let's look into how journaling can be a powerful tool for reframing your thoughts and deepening your mental clarity. Through guided prompts, you'll learn to uncover hidden beliefs, challenge negative patterns, and rewrite the stories that no longer serve you. For now, take a moment to reflect: *What small practice can you begin today to create space for clarity in your life?* The journey to a clearer mind begins with a single step—and the possibilities are limitless

Journaling Prompts to Reframe Your Thoughts

Journaling is more than just writing—it's a mirror for your mind, a safe space to explore your thoughts, and a tool to reshape the narratives that hold you back. When you put pen to paper, you invite clarity, insight, and healing into your life. Your thoughts, once scattered and overwhelming, become organized and manageable. Journaling isn't about perfect grammar or eloquent sentences; it's about giving yourself permission to process, reflect, and transform.

Reframing your thoughts through journaling starts with the right questions.

These prompts act as a gentle guide, encouraging you to dig deeper into your beliefs, identify patterns, and uncover truths that may have been hidden beneath the surface. They're not just questions; they're invitations to grow, to see things differently, and to rewrite the stories you tell yourself.

One powerful journaling prompt is to ask yourself, *"What thought has been weighing on me today, and is it based on fact or fear?"* This question helps you see things as they truly are, rather than how your mind might exaggerate them. Write down the thought and then challenge it. Is there evidence to support it, or is it rooted in assumptions and worst-case scenarios? Often, you'll find that the thought loses its power when brought into the light of reason.

Another transformative prompt is, *"What is the story I'm telling myself about this situation?"* Once you understand the story being told, you can start to evaluate its truthfulness. For example, if you're facing a setback and your inner dialogue says, *"I'll never succeed,"* ask yourself: *"Is this true? "How can I support or refute this claim?"* This process helps replace limiting beliefs with empowering ones.

Gratitude journaling can also reframe your thoughts. Begin with the prompt, *"What are three things I'm grateful for today?"* Shifting your focus from what's missing to what's present, gratitude cultivates a sense of abundance and peace. Even on challenging days, finding small moments of gratitude—like a kind word from a friend or the beauty of a sunset—can help you see life through a more positive lens.

When you're feeling stuck, try the prompt, *"What would I say to a friend in my situation?"* This allows you to access your own wisdom by stepping outside your perspective. We often show more kindness and support to others than we do to ourselves. By framing the situation as if you're offering advice to someone else, you can uncover solutions and self-compassion.

Journaling can also help you clarify your goals and intentions. Use the prompt, *"What do I want to create in my life, and what steps can I take to move closer to it?"* Not only does writing down your desires clarify them, but it also breaks them down into actionable steps. It transforms abstract dreams into achievable plans.

If you find yourself overwhelmed by self-doubt, explore the question, *"What fear is holding me back, and how can I move through it?"* Uncertainty breeds fear, but once we identify and face it, its power diminishes. Pair this with the follow-up prompt, *"What is one small action I can take today to move past this fear?"* Even the smallest actions can boost confidence and propel progress.

To deepen your self-awareness, ask, *"What did I learn about myself today?"* This question encourages reflection and helps you see each day as a step in your growth. Whether it's a strength you discovered or a habit you want to change, this practice keeps you connected to your journey.

When you're facing a decision, try the prompt, *"What does my intuition say, and what does my fear say?"*

Writing this helps differentiate between wisdom's quiet voice and anxiety's louder one. Trusting your intuition becomes easier when you see its clarity on the page.

Finally, use the prompt, "What story am I ready to let go of?" to encourage yourself to abandon limiting beliefs and outdated narratives. Whether it's a belief about your worth, a fear of failure, or a pattern of negative thinking, letting go of these stories creates space for new ones that align with who you want to become.

As you journal, don't censor yourself. Let the words flow freely, even if they don't make sense at first. This practice is for you—there's no right or wrong way to do it. Over time, you'll notice patterns emerging, clarity increasing, and a deeper connection to your inner self.

Journaling isn't just a tool for mental clarity; it's a way to reclaim your power over your thoughts and reshape your inner world. Each entry is a step toward freedom, a small act of courage that brings you closer to the life you desire.

Next, we'll discuss how mindfulness techniques that help you balance your emotions and cultivate inner peace. These practices, combined with journaling, create a powerful toolkit for navigating life's challenges with grace. For now, take a moment to reflect on this question: *What thought or belief am I ready to challenge today?* Let your answer guide your next journal entry—it could be the start of a transformation you never imagined.

Mindfulness Techniques for Emotional Balance

Mindfulness is more than just a trendy concept; it's a life-altering practice that brings you back to the present moment, grounding you in reality instead of the chaos of your thoughts. Emotional balance isn't about suppressing feelings or pretending to be unaffected by life's challenges. It's about learning to experience emotions fully, without letting them take control of your actions or mental state. By cultivating mindfulness, you develop the ability to observe your emotions with curiosity and compassion, allowing them to flow through you rather than getting stuck within you.

One of the simplest yet most profound mindfulness techniques is breath awareness. Your breath is always with you, a steady rhythm anchoring you to the present. Start by sitting comfortably and taking a few deep breaths, inhaling through your nose and exhaling through your mouth Afterwards, allow your breathing to return to its normal pace. Focus your attention on the sensation of air entering and leaving your body. Notice the rise and fall of your chest, the coolness of the air as it touches your nostrils, and the warmth as you exhale. If your mind starts to wander, bring your attention back to your breath. This practice is not about controlling your thoughts but about redirecting your focus, over and over, with patience and kindness.

Body scanning is another powerful mindfulness exercise. It involves systematically bringing your attention to different parts of your body, noticing any sensations, tension, or areas of relaxation. Begin at the top of your head and slowly move downward, pausing at your shoulders, chest, abdomen, and so on, until you reach your feet. As you scan, try not to judge what you feel; simply observe it. This technique helps you tune into your body's signals and release tension you may not even realize you're holding.

Mindful observation is an excellent practice for reconnecting with your surroundings and calming an overactive mind. Choose an object around you—a flower, a cup of tea, or even your own hand. Focus your attention entirely on this object. Notice its texture, color, shape, and any other details that catch your eye. Allow yourself to be fully present with it, as if you're seeing it for the first time. This practice pulls you out of your racing thoughts and into the vividness of the present moment.

When emotions feel overwhelming, try the "Name It to Tame It" technique. This entails identifying and naming the emotions you are experiencing. For example, if you feel anxious, say to yourself, "I am noticing anxiety." If you're angry, "I am noticing anger." By naming the emotion, you create a sense of separation between yourself and the feeling, reminding you that you are not your emotions—they are temporary experiences passing through you.

Another practice that fosters emotional balance is mindful journaling. Unlike structured journaling prompts, this technique involves free writing with an emphasis on emotional awareness. Set a timer for 10 minutes, and without stopping to edit or overthink, write down whatever is on your mind. Let the words flow, capturing your thoughts and feelings as they arise. When the timer ends, read through what you've written with an attitude of curiosity rather than judgment. This exercise helps you process emotions and gain insight into patterns that may be affecting your mental state.

For moments when stress feels unmanageable, a grounding exercise like the 5-4-3-2-1 technique can help. You need to find five things you can see, four things you can feel, three things you can hear, two things you can smell, and one thing you can taste. By engaging your senses, you shift your focus away from spiraling thoughts and reconnect with your immediate environment.

Loving-kindness meditation is another technique that cultivates emotional balance by fostering compassion toward yourself and others. Start by silently repeating phrases such as "May I be happy, healthy, and peaceful." Then, extend these wishes to others, beginning with a loved one, followed by someone neutral, and finally someone you find challenging. This practice softens feelings of anger, resentment, or self-criticism, replacing them with understanding and connection.

Incorporating mindfulness into your daily routine doesn't require hours of meditation or complex rituals. You can practice mindfulness while washing dishes, walking, or even brushing your teeth. The key is to focus entirely on the task at hand, bringing your full attention to the sensations, movements, and details of the experience.

As you begin to integrate these techniques into your life, you'll notice a shift. Moments that once felt overwhelming start to feel manageable. Emotions that once controlled you become easier to navigate. You build a resilience that allows you to face life's challenges with greater calm and clarity. Mindfulness doesn't eliminate difficulties; it equips you to meet them with grace.

In the next chapter, we'll explore the transformative power of letting go and living fully in the present. What does it mean to release the weight of the past and the anxiety of the future? How can you embrace the beauty of this moment without being held back by fear or regret? For now, take a deep breath and reflect: *What would it feel like to live each day with greater peace and balance?* The answer is already within you, just waiting to be discovered.

Chapter 12: Letting Go and Living in the Present

Letting go and living in the present is not about erasing your past or ignoring your future—it's about reclaiming your power over the only moment you truly have: now. This is where life happens, where opportunities unfold, and where your choices shape the reality you live in. Yet so many of us are trapped in a cycle of dwelling on what was or worrying about what might be, missing the richness of the present moment entirely.

The art of letting go begins with understanding that the past is a memory, and the future is a projection. Both exist only in your mind, yet they often feel more real than the life happening around you. How often have you replayed a painful memory, dissecting every detail, only to feel the same sting of regret or shame as if it were happening all over again? Or how frequently have you fretted about an imagined scenario, convincing yourself it was inevitable, only to realize later that it never came to pass? These patterns not only steal your peace but also rob you of the chance to experience the beauty of the now.

To live fully in the present, you must practice releasing your grip on what you cannot control. This doesn't mean ignoring your responsibilities or goals—it means shifting your focus to what you can do in this moment to create a life you love.

Letting go is not giving up; it's giving yourself the freedom to respond to life with clarity and intention, unburdened by the weight of unnecessary suffering.

One way to anchor yourself in the present is to embrace the power of attention. What you focus on grows, so when your attention is consumed by regrets or anxieties, those feelings magnify. Instead, try this: pick a single thing to focus on in your immediate environment. It could be the warmth of the sun on your skin, the sound of the wind rustling through the trees, or the sensation of your feet touching the ground. Let yourself become fully absorbed in this experience. Feel the simplicity and peace of being here, now.

Another key to living in the present is accepting uncertainty. Life is inherently unpredictable, and the need to control every outcome is a futile pursuit that drains your energy and diminishes your joy. Instead of fighting against uncertainty, try embracing it. Trust that not knowing what comes next is part of the adventure, a chance to grow and discover things you never imagined. When you release the need for certainty, you make room for possibility.

Letting go also involves forgiving yourself and others. Carrying resentment or guilt ties you to the past and keeps you from moving forward. Forgiveness doesn't mean condoning harmful behavior; it means freeing yourself from the emotional chains that bind you to it. Start small.

Identify one grievance you're holding onto and ask yourself, *What would it feel like to let this go?* Imagine how much lighter your heart would be without carrying that burden.

Living in the present also means embracing impermanence. Everything in life is temporary—your struggles, your triumphs, even your emotions. This isn't a reason to despair; it's a reminder to cherish what you have while you have it. The fleeting nature of life gives every moment its value. Instead of fearing change, see it as a natural rhythm, an invitation to grow and adapt.

A practical exercise for staying present is to create a daily grounding ritual. Set aside a few minutes each morning to breathe deeply, express gratitude, or simply sit in silence. Use this time to center yourself and remind yourself of your intention to live mindfully throughout the day. These small practices, done consistently, build the foundation for a life rooted in the present.

Letting go and living in the present is not a destination but a practice. There will be days when your mind pulls you back into old patterns of worry or regret, and that's okay. Each time you catch yourself drifting, gently guide your attention back to the now. Over time, this practice becomes second nature, and you'll find yourself living with greater ease, clarity, and joy.

Imagine the possibilities if you were no longer tethered to the past or paralyzed by the future. What could you create?

Who could you become? The answers lie not in some distant moment but right here, right now.

In the next section, we'll explore how to break free from the endless cycle of worrying about what has already happened or what might come next. How do you silence the "what-ifs" and "if-onlys" that cloud your mind? The path forward begins with a simple but profound shift, one that will open the door to peace and freedom. For now, take a deep breath and let this moment remind you of what it feels like to truly live.

How to Stop Worrying About the Past or Future

Worrying about the past or future is like carrying an invisible weight that grows heavier with each step. It saps your energy, clouds your mind, and disconnects you from the life happening around you. Yet, the pull of worry feels almost magnetic, as if obsessing over past mistakes or trying to predict the future might somehow offer control or safety. But the truth is, it never does.

Worry thrives on uncertainty. When you replay a moment from the past, it's rarely with clarity or neutrality. Instead, your mind attaches judgments, reimagining what you could have said or done differently, crafting an alternate reality where you were somehow "better."

Similarly, when you project into the future, you often do so from a place of fear, imagining scenarios that feed your anxiety rather than provide solutions. This endless loop keeps you stuck, spinning in mental chaos instead of living in peace.

Breaking free from this cycle requires a radical shift in how you relate to your thoughts. You can't control what pops into your mind, but you can decide how much power you give it. The first step is recognizing when you're caught in the trap of worry. Pay attention to the physical sensations that accompany these moments—tightness in your chest, a racing heart, or shallow breathing. These are your body's cues, signaling that your mind has wandered to places that aren't serving you.

Once you've noticed the pattern, practice separating the thought from reality. Ask yourself, *Is this thought a fact, or is it a story I'm telling myself?* Often, worries are rooted in assumptions, not truths. For instance, replaying a conversation where you fear you came across poorly might feel urgent, but it's based on your interpretation, not the other person's reality. Recognizing this helps loosen worry's grip.

Another powerful technique is what psychologists call "grounding." When you feel overwhelmed by thoughts of the past or future, anchor yourself in the present moment. This could be as simple as naming five things you see around you, focusing on the sensation of your feet on the ground, or taking a deep breath and noticing the rise and fall of your chest. These small acts bring you back to the only reality you can influence—the now.

Letting go of worry also requires a mindset shift. Accept that the past is unchangeable, no matter how much mental energy you pour into it. Use that energy instead to reflect on what you've learned and how you can grow. The future, while unpredictable, is shaped by the choices you make today. Worry doesn't prevent bad things from happening; it only robs you of the strength to deal with them if they do. When you focus on what's within your control—your actions and responses in this moment—you reclaim your power.

A practical exercise for releasing worry about the future is to write down your fears. Seeing them on paper often diminishes their power and reveals their irrationality. Once you've listed them, divide them into two categories: things you can control and things you can't. For the things you can control, make a small, actionable plan to address them. For the things you can't, remind yourself that worrying won't change the outcome. Then, consciously let them go. You might even visualize placing them in a box and setting it aside.

Cultivating gratitude is another antidote to worry. When your mind is consumed by what-ifs or if-onlys, pause and ask yourself, *What is good about this moment?* Gratitude shifts your focus from what's missing to what's present, grounding you in appreciation rather than lack. It's nearly impossible to feel deep gratitude and overwhelming worry simultaneously.

Imagine what your life could look like without the constant burden of past regrets or future fears. How much lighter would your days feel?

How much more joy could you experience? These aren't just rhetorical questions—they're invitations to step into a new way of being, one where worry doesn't dictate your decisions or define your experiences.

As you let go of the past and release your grip on the future, you'll find that the present holds more than enough to sustain you. It's where your strength lies, where your dreams take shape, and where your life unfolds.

Next, we'll delve into the beauty of simplicity and how embracing it can bring profound inner peace. Sometimes, less truly is more, and learning to simplify your thoughts, environment, and priorities can open the door to a calmer, more fulfilling life. Keep reading to discover how letting go of complexity can help you create a clearer, more intentional path forward.

Embracing Simplicity for Inner Peace

Simplicity is often misunderstood in today's world, where complexity is equated with success and busyness with productivity. But the truth is, simplicity is not about deprivation or minimalism for the sake of aesthetics. It's about clarity. It's about stripping away the excess noise, distractions, and unnecessary burdens that prevent you from being fully present and at peace with yourself.

At its core, simplicity is the antidote to overwhelm.

When your mind is cluttered with obligations, expectations, and the constant need to prove yourself, peace becomes an impossible goal. Embracing simplicity means taking a step back and asking yourself, *What truly matters?* It's a question that clears the fog and reveals the essentials—the relationships, pursuits, and moments that bring genuine joy and fulfillment.

Simplicity begins with your thoughts. Every day, your mind generates countless worries, comparisons, and judgments, most of which serve no purpose but to complicate your experience. The practice of simplifying your inner dialogue is not about silencing your mind but about discerning what deserves your attention. When a thought arises, ask yourself, *Is this useful? Does this contribute to my peace or my growth?* If the answer is no, gently let it go. The act of deciding what to hold onto and what to release is a form of self-care.

Your environment, too, reflects your mental state. Look around you: Is your space filled with things that drain your energy rather than nurture it? Physical clutter often mirrors mental clutter. Simplifying your surroundings—whether it's organizing a chaotic desk or letting go of items you no longer need—can have a profound effect on your sense of peace. Each item you release is a reminder that your worth is not tied to possessions or appearances but to the life you are creating.

Simplicity also applies to your time. In a culture that glorifies busyness, it's easy to say yes to everything out of fear of missing out or disappointing others.

But every yes is also a no to something else—often to yourself. Protect your time fiercely. When you simplify your commitments, you make space for the moments that nourish your soul, whether it's a quiet walk, meaningful conversation, or time to simply be.

Practicing simplicity requires courage. It asks you to let go of the need to control every detail, the fear of not doing enough, and the pressure to keep up with others. But in that letting go, you gain something far more valuable: freedom. Freedom to experience the present moment without distraction. Freedom to connect with your true self and what matters most. The freedom to live authentically and true to oneself.

Imagine waking up each day with a sense of ease, unburdened by the chaos that used to weigh you down. This isn't an impossible dream; it's the reality that simplicity offers. And while it takes effort to cultivate, the rewards are profound. A simpler life is not just a quieter life; it's a richer one, filled with the clarity and peace that come from focusing on what truly matters.

As you simplify your thoughts, your surroundings, and your commitments, you'll notice something remarkable: the world doesn't collapse when you stop trying to do it all. Instead, it expands. You begin to see beauty in the small, ordinary moments that once passed unnoticed. You start to feel the fullness of life in the spaces you once thought were empty.

Living simply is not a destination but a practice—a commitment to choosing peace over perfection and presence over productivity. It's a journey of discovering that the life you've always wanted doesn't require more; it requires less. Less noise. Less striving. Less worry. And in that space, the light of your true self shines through, illuminating the path to a life of deeper meaning and joy.

As we move forward, we'll explore an even more profound concept: unconditional joy. How do you cultivate happiness that isn't tied to circumstances, possessions, or achievements? What does it mean to find joy that endures through life's challenges and uncertainties? In the next chapter, we'll uncover the secrets to living with a sense of unshakable contentment and fulfillment, no matter what life brings.

Chapter 13: The Path to Unconditional Joy

Unconditional joy is a concept that seems almost mythical in a world conditioned to believe that happiness is a fleeting reward for achieving external milestones. We're taught to tether our joy to a promotion, a relationship, a financial windfall, or even the approval of others. Yet, as you simplify your life and begin to let go of the imaginary constraints you've been living under, a profound realization starts to emerge: true joy isn't something you earn. It's something you uncover.

Joy exists not in the highs of success or the relief of a problem solved, but in the quiet moments of connection—with yourself, with others, and with life itself. It's the state of being that arises when you stop chasing happiness and begin to experience the richness of the present. But to reach this place, you must first dismantle the belief that joy is conditional.

The first step toward unconditional joy is recognizing that external circumstances do not create it. The biggest myth you've been sold is that something outside of you holds the key to your happiness. When you believe this, you become a hostage to an endless cycle of striving—always chasing, never arriving. One job isn't enough, one relationship doesn't feel complete, one moment of success is overshadowed by the desire for more. This isn't living; it's a perpetual state of waiting.

Unconditional joy invites you to release the waiting game. It asks you to shift your focus from what's missing to what's already present.

Even now, at this moment, there is something to appreciate—a breath, a memory, a small comfort. Joy doesn't demand perfection; it asks for presence. When you stop looking for joy in grand gestures and start noticing it in the subtle details of life, you realize it was never absent. You simply weren't paying attention.

Another critical piece of the puzzle is letting go of the need for control. Much of our suffering stems from the illusion that we can—or must—manage every aspect of our lives to feel secure or happy. Unconditional joy thrives in the opposite environment. It grows when you relinquish control and trust in the flow of life. This isn't passive resignation; it's active surrender. It's knowing that even when life doesn't go as planned, you can still find peace and purpose within yourself.

Practically, cultivating unconditional joy begins with small, deliberate actions. Start each day by identifying one thing you're grateful for—not out of obligation but as a reminder of what's already good in your life. Gratitude is the gateway to joy because it anchors you in the present and shifts your perspective from lack to abundance. Another step is to engage in activities that light you up—not because they're productive or valuable in the eyes of others, but because they bring you alive. We need joy as much as we need anything else.

Equally important is the practice of self-compassion. Unconditional joy cannot coexist with constant self-criticism. Treat yourself as you would a dear friend, offering kindness and understanding instead of judgment.

When you allow yourself to be imperfect and human, you open the door to joy. You begin to perceive that you are deserving of happiness, unconditionally.

Unconditional joy also requires a redefinition of success. Instead of measuring your worth by achievements or outcomes, measure it by your ability to stay connected to your inner peace, regardless of what's happening around you. True success isn't about having more; it's about needing less. When you redefine success in these terms, joy becomes an inevitable byproduct rather than an elusive goal.

As you walk this path, you'll encounter resistance—old habits, lingering doubts, and the ever-present lure of external validation. This is normal. But each time you choose joy over fear, presence over distraction, and gratitude over complaint, you reinforce the truth that joy is your birthright. It's not something you have to fight for; it's something you remember.

The journey to unconditional joy is not about transforming your circumstances but transforming your relationship with them. It's about seeing the beauty in what is, rather than waiting for what could be. It's about understanding that joy isn't fragile; it's resilient. And so are you.

As we move forward, we'll explore how this mindset can extend to every area of your life. In the next section, we'll delve into creating a mindset of abundance and flow—a perspective that not only nurtures joy but also opens the door to limitless possibilities.

Imagine a life where opportunities seem to come effortlessly, where you feel in harmony with your true self, and where joy isn't just a fleeting moment but a steady current. That's where we're headed next.

Creating a Mindset of Abundance and Flow

A mindset of abundance and flow is not just a feel-good concept; it's a transformative way of engaging with life. Imagine waking up each day with the quiet confidence that you already have enough, that you are enough, and that life itself is working with you rather than against you. This isn't wishful thinking—it's a recalibration of your mental and emotional lens. When you shift from scarcity to abundance and from rigidity to flow, you open doors to possibilities that were once hidden by fear and self-doubt.

The first step toward cultivating this mindset is recognizing the narrative of scarcity that dominates much of our thinking. Scarcity isn't just about money or material possessions; it's the belief that there's not enough—time, love, opportunities, or even worthiness. This belief drives comparison, envy, and an insatiable need to prove yourself. But scarcity is a lie. Abundance, by contrast, is the truth of existence. Look at nature—there's no lack of beauty, growth, or renewal. When you align yourself with this principle, you begin to see the world not as a place of limitations but as a canvas of opportunities.

Flow, on the other hand, is the natural state of being when you let go of resistance. It's not about forcing outcomes or controlling every detail of your life. It's about trusting that life unfolds in perfect timing, even when it doesn't follow your plan. Flow doesn't mean passivity; it means engaged presence. When you're in flow, you act with intention, but you're not attached to results. This balance of effort and surrender creates harmony, not just within you but in how you interact with the world.

Creating this mindset begins with awareness. Pay attention to how often you think in terms of "not enough." Not enough money, not enough time, not enough talent, not enough progress. Then challenge those thoughts. Ask yourself: Is this true, or is it just a story I've been telling myself? Often, the very things you think you lack are already within your reach, but you've been too consumed by doubt to notice.

Gratitude is a powerful tool for abundance. It's not about ignoring what you want or settling for less; it's about acknowledging what's already good in your life. Gratitude shifts your focus from lack to plenty. Start a daily practice of writing down three things you're thankful for. They don't have to be monumental—small joys, like a kind word from a friend or the warmth of sunlight, are just as significant. Over time, this practice rewires your brain to see the abundance that's always been there.

Flow, too, can be cultivated through mindfulness and trust.

When faced with a challenge, resist the urge to overthink or control every variable. Take the next logical step, confident that the path will become clearer as you move forward. Flow isn't about having all the answers; it's about being open to them as they arise.

Another critical aspect of this mindset is detaching your sense of self-worth from external outcomes. Abundance and flow thrive when you know that your value doesn't depend on your achievements, your possessions, or the opinions of others. Practice affirmations like, "I am enough as I am," or "My worth is inherent, not earned." These simple statements, repeated daily, can begin to dismantle the deep-seated belief that you must constantly strive to prove your value.

Embracing abundance and flow also means redefining success. Instead of measuring it by traditional markers like wealth or status, measure it by how aligned you feel with your true self. Are you living authentically? Are your choices guided by joy rather than fear? When you use these metrics, you'll find that success and fulfillment are not things you chase but things you embody.

This transformation won't happen overnight Just like any new habit, it requires consistent practice and patience. There will be days when scarcity thinking creeps back in, when flow feels elusive. But each time you choose abundance over fear, trust over control, and gratitude over lack, you're strengthening this mindset. You're teaching yourself to live in a state of openness, possibility, and peace.

Imagine a life where you're no longer paralyzed by the fear of not having enough or being enough. Picture the freedom of knowing that you're supported by an abundant universe and that your efforts, combined with trust, will always lead you to where you need to be. This is the power of abundance and flow, and it's available to you right now.

As we move forward, we'll explore how this mindset can anchor you in peace, regardless of external circumstances. In the next section, we'll dive into how to find calm and stability even when life feels chaotic. Get ready to uncover the kind of inner peace that not only survives challenges but thrives in their midst.

Finding Peace Regardless of Circumstances

Finding peace regardless of circumstances is one of life's most liberating achievements. It's not about living in denial of challenges or forcing positivity when everything feels heavy. Instead, it's about cultivating a deep, unshakable calm that doesn't rely on external validation, outcomes, or conditions. Peace, at its core, is an internal state—a sanctuary you can retreat to no matter what is happening around you.

One of the most significant barriers to finding peace is the belief that it is tied to everything going right. This mindset creates a constant pursuit of control, a futile attempt to bend life to our will.

But life is inherently unpredictable, and trying to control it all only leads to frustration and exhaustion. True peace comes when we release the need to control and instead embrace the present as it is, trusting that we have the resilience to face whatever unfolds.

This doesn't mean passivity or resignation. Accepting circumstances doesn't mean you approve of them—it means you acknowledge their reality without allowing them to define your emotional state. Acceptance is the gateway to clarity. When you stop fighting against what is, your energy shifts from resistance to response. You move from "Why is this happening to me?" to "What can I do now?"

Finding peace also requires stepping away from the stories your mind spins about how things *should* be. The word "should" is a trap, often rooted in comparison and unmet expectations. It clouds your ability to see what *is* and to appreciate the lessons and growth available in the moment. Begin to replace "should" with curiosity. Instead of "This shouldn't be happening," try asking, "What can this teach me? How can I grow through this?" Curiosity transforms frustration into possibility.

Another key to peace is recognizing that your worth isn't dictated by your circumstances. External events don't diminish your value, and they don't add to it, either. This understanding allows you to detach your sense of self from what happens around you. When your identity isn't tethered to outcomes or others' opinions, you gain the freedom to remain centered, regardless of external chaos.

Gratitude is a powerful practice in cultivating peace. It shifts your focus from what's wrong to what's right, even in difficult times. Gratitude doesn't erase pain, but it anchors you in the present, where beauty still exists. Each day, pause to reflect on something that brings you a sense of grounding—whether it's a supportive friend, the stillness of a morning, or the resilience you've discovered within yourself. Over time, this practice rewires your mind to seek peace rather than dwell on worry.

Breathwork and mindfulness are practical tools for anchoring yourself in peace. When anxiety threatens to pull you into a spiral, close your eyes and take slow, deliberate breaths. Inhale deeply, counting to four, hold for four, and exhale for six. This practice activates your body's relaxation response, reminding you that in this moment, you are safe. Pair this with mindfulness—observing your thoughts and surroundings without judgment. Notice the warmth of sunlight on your skin or the sound of the wind through the trees. These small moments tether you to the present, where peace resides.

Finally, let go of the need to be "perfectly peaceful." The pursuit of perfection in any form only creates stress. Peace isn't a destination; it's a practice. Some days, it will feel effortless, and other days, it will feel elusive. Both are okay. The goal isn't to eliminate discomfort but to coexist with it, knowing it doesn't define you. Trust that even in moments of struggle, peace is still available—it's simply waiting for you to remember it.

Imagine being liberated from the constraints of circumstance. Picture yourself moving through life with a steady inner calm, unshaken by the storms that once overwhelmed you. This is not just a possibility; it's a reality you can create with consistent practice and intention.

As we prepare to conclude this journey, remember that finding peace is not the end of the road—it's the foundation for the life you've always desired. In the final chapter, we'll bring together all the threads we've explored and chart a course for what comes next. This is where your journey truly begins. Get ready to step into a life of clarity, joy, and unshakable freedom. The best is yet to come. Keep reading—you won't want to miss the closing reflections that tie everything together and propel you forward.

Conclusion: Your Journey Begins Here

Your journey toward freedom—true, lasting freedom—has only just begun. As you reflect on the path you've walked through these pages, you've probably noticed something shifting inside you. Maybe it's the weight of overthinking lifting ever so slightly. Perhaps it's the subtle realization that you don't have to believe every thought that passes through your mind. Or maybe it's the growing confidence that your life can be guided by clarity, peace, and joy rather than fear and self-doubt.

Each chapter has peeled back a layer of the mental barriers that once seemed insurmountable. You've explored the depths of your imagination, learned how it can both liberate and imprison you, and discovered practical ways to break free from the cycle of limiting beliefs. You've journeyed into the heart of what it means to live in the present, cultivate emotional resilience, and embrace a mindset of abundance. And now, you stand at a powerful crossroads—a moment where understanding meets action, and where your new life begins.

The first and most crucial step forward is to realize that this isn't about fixing yourself. You were never broken. The overthinking, the self-doubt, the fear—those were simply learned patterns, not reflections of your true essence. Beneath those layers lies a part of you that has always been whole, capable, and ready to thrive.

This journey isn't about becoming someone else; it's about uncovering who you've always been beneath the noise of your mind.

The tools you've gathered are not one-time solutions but lifelong companions. The next time your thoughts spiral into a storm of "what-ifs," you'll remember how to pause, breathe, and ground yourself in the present. When fear whispers that you're not enough, you'll challenge it with curiosity rather than letting it define your reality. And when life throws uncertainty your way, you'll lean into it, knowing that every challenge carries the seed of growth and transformation.

But freedom is not a destination—it's a practice. There will be days when the old habits of overthinking and self-doubt resurface, but those moments are not setbacks; they're opportunities. Each time you choose to respond with awareness rather than reactivity, you strengthen your capacity to live freely. Each small victory compounds, creating a ripple effect that transforms not just your inner world but also your relationships, choices, and experiences.

The life you're stepping into is one of empowerment. It's a life where you no longer wait for external circumstances to grant you permission to feel joy, peace, or fulfillment. Instead, you claim those experiences as your birthright, independent of the highs and lows of the world around you. You've learned that your thoughts don't have to hold you captive. Now, you're ready to wield your mind as a tool for creation rather than as a source of suffering.

Take a moment to imagine what's possible from here. Picture yourself waking up each morning not with dread or anxiety but with curiosity and gratitude for the day ahead. Visualize moving through challenges with grace, not because they're easy, but because you trust in your ability to navigate them. Envision a life where your goals align with your values, where your relationships are nourished by presence and authenticity, and where you embrace every moment—messy, imperfect, and beautiful—for what it is.

The journey ahead is yours to shape. Every choice you make from this point forward is an opportunity to step into your power and rewrite the narrative of your life. The road may not always be smooth, but you've already proven your resilience. You've shown yourself that transformation is possible, and that alone is a triumph worth celebrating.

As we close this chapter together, remember that the path to freedom is illuminated by awareness and intention. Every breath, every decision, every thought is a chance to practice living in alignment with the person you're becoming. Your journey begins here—not with a perfect plan, but with the courage to take the first step and then the next.

In the pages to come, we'll delve deeper into what it means to live with awareness and intention. This final exploration will tie together all the insights you've gained and offer practical ways to sustain your transformation.

Living with Awareness and Intention

Living with awareness and intention is not a single act or a milestone to reach; it's a way of being, a conscious decision made in every moment to choose presence over distraction and purpose over autopilot. It's the art of stepping into your life fully, not as an observer dragged along by circumstances, but as an active participant who holds the pen to their own story. This isn't about living perfectly—it's about living truthfully, with your values and desires aligned.

Awareness begins with paying attention, not just to what's happening around you, but to what's happening within. How often do we move through our days on autopilot, reacting out of habit rather than responding with intention? Perhaps you've noticed it in your own life: the way you reach for your phone when an uncomfortable thought arises, or the way you avoid a difficult conversation because it's easier to bury the discomfort. These small moments are where transformation happens. Living with awareness means catching yourself in those moments and asking, "Is this what I want? Is this action serving the life I'm trying to create?"

It might sound simple, but awareness is radical because it disrupts the unconscious patterns that have governed your life. It shines a light on the beliefs you've carried without question, the stories you've told yourself about who you are and what you're capable of.

And when those stories no longer align with the truth, awareness gives you the power to rewrite them. It's the space between a thought and a reaction, between an old belief and a new possibility.

Once awareness lays the foundation, intention takes the lead. Intention is the bridge between knowing and doing, between recognizing what matters and actually living in alignment with it. It's not about striving for perfection or setting rigid rules; it's about choosing your direction with clarity and purpose. Intention gives meaning to your actions, no matter how small. It transforms mundane tasks into opportunities to practice presence and gratitude. It turns challenges into invitations to grow.

For example, imagine waking up tomorrow and setting a simple intention for your day. It could be to approach your work with focus, to listen more deeply to a loved one, or to take five minutes to breathe when you feel overwhelmed. The act of setting that intention anchors you in the present, reminding you of your power to shape your experience. It's not about controlling every outcome; it's about showing up with clarity and heart.

Living intentionally also means saying no—to distractions, to obligations that don't align with your values, to the internal pressure to be everything to everyone. It's about creating space in your life for what truly matters, even if it means disappointing others or letting go of old patterns. This is not selfishness; this is self-respect. Every time you say no to what drains you, you say yes to what fills you.

Every time you choose intention over obligation, you reclaim a piece of your freedom.

As you begin to live with more awareness and intention, you'll notice shifts—not just in your mindset but in your entire being. Decisions become clearer, relationships deepen, and life feels less like a series of hurdles to overcome and more like an unfolding journey. The beauty of this practice is that it doesn't require drastic changes or external circumstances to align. It starts here, right now, in the smallest of moments.

Take a deep breath. Feel the air fill your lungs and remind yourself that this moment is all there ever truly is. What you choose to do with it is where your power lies. The past is a memory; the future, a possibility. But this moment? This is where life happens. Living with awareness and intention is the practice of honoring this truth, again and again, until it becomes second nature.

As we close this chapter of exploration, consider this: What would your life look like if you approached every day with a sense of purpose? What would it feel like to trust yourself to handle whatever comes your way, not with fear but with confidence and grace? These are not rhetorical questions—they are invitations. The answers lie not in your thoughts but in your actions.

In the final subchapter of this journey, we'll explore how to sustain the changes you've made and continue growing into the person you're becoming. Transformation is not a one-time event; it's a lifelong process, and every step forward builds upon the last. Together, we'll uncover the tools and mindset needed to embrace this evolution fully. Stay with me. The best is yet to come.

How to Sustain Change and Continue Growing

Change is often seen as a single event, a moment when everything shifts and you suddenly become the person you've always wanted to be. But the truth is, change is rarely dramatic—it's subtle, often invisible at first, and always ongoing. Sustaining change and continuing to grow is not about chasing a finish line; it's about building a foundation for a life that reflects your deepest values and truest self. It's a journey of committing to progress, not perfection, and embracing the lessons along the way.

The first step to sustaining change is understanding that transformation is a practice, not a destination. Just like physical exercise, mental and emotional growth requires consistent effort. There will be days when it feels easy, and days when it feels like a battle. Both are part of the process. When setbacks arise—and they will—they are not failures but reminders to realign with your purpose. The beauty of growth lies in the willingness to begin again, no matter how many times it's needed.

One way to anchor this practice is through rituals that align with the person you're becoming. These rituals can be simple and brief, as long as they are deliberate. Maybe it's a morning moment of gratitude that reminds you of what truly matters, or an evening reflection on what went well and what you've learned. These small acts create momentum, reinforcing your commitment to live differently.

Equally important is the company you keep. Surround yourself with people who inspire you, challenge you, and celebrate your growth. Relationships are one of the most powerful influences on your mindset and behavior, and choosing to spend time with those who uplift you is an act of self-respect. This doesn't mean cutting ties with anyone who isn't on the same path, but rather prioritizing connections that nurture your growth.

Another essential aspect of sustaining change is cultivating patience with yourself. Growth often feels chaotic because it requires venturing into the unknown, which can be unsettling. But discomfort is not a sign that you're on the wrong path—it's a sign that you're evolving. Embrace your unfinished journey. Celebrate small victories and trust that every step, no matter how small, is leading you closer to the life you desire.

To continue growing, you must remain curious. Ask yourself questions that expand your perspective: What can I learn from this experience? How can I approach this challenge with creativity instead of fear?

Curiosity keeps you open to new possibilities and helps you avoid falling back into old patterns. It transforms obstacles into opportunities and setbacks into stepping stones.

Perhaps most importantly, let go of the need for constant validation. True growth doesn't come from external approval; it comes from within. When you stop seeking permission to be yourself, you create space for authentic joy and fulfillment. You learn to trust your own judgment and to find peace in your choices, even when they defy expectations.

Sustaining change also means forgiving yourself when you stumble. Old habits may resurface, and limiting beliefs may try to creep back in. This is normal—it's part of being human. What matters is not avoiding mistakes but how you respond to them. Meet yourself with compassion, remind yourself of your progress, and take the next step forward.

As you reach the end of this book, you might feel a mix of emotions: hope, excitement, maybe even a little apprehension about what lies ahead. That's okay. The path to breaking free from limiting beliefs and transforming your life is not linear, but it is worth every step. You're not going through this alone. Every person who has ever dared to challenge their inner narrative has walked a similar path, and they've proven that it's possible to rewrite the story.

Your journey begins here, in this moment, with the awareness that you hold the power to create a life beyond limits. The lessons and tools in this book are not the end—they are the beginning. They are the foundation for a life that reflects the truth of who you are and the freedom to live in alignment with that truth.

As you step into this new phase of your life, carry this thought with you: Every day is an opportunity to choose growth, to let go of what no longer serves you, and to embrace the endless possibilities that await. The path forward is yours to create, and with each step, you'll find that the limits you once believed in are nothing more than illusions.

Thank you for sharing this journey. The next chapter of your life is waiting—one where you no longer believe everything you imagine but instead live with clarity, courage, and intention. Let this be your first step into a life of freedom, joy, and boundless potential. Your journey begins here.

Thank You!!!

Dear Reader,

Thank you for choosing to spend your valuable time with *Don't Believe Everything You Imagine: Break Free from Limiting Beliefs and Transform Your Life*. Writing this book has been a deeply personal and rewarding journey, and knowing it has made its way into your hands fills me with gratitude.

I hope the words on these pages have sparked something meaningful within you—whether it's a new perspective, a moment of clarity, or a sense of hope for the future. You've taken an important step by committing to your personal growth, and I honor your courage in facing the inner work required to break free and live life on your terms.

Your journey doesn't end here. The lessons, tools, and insights shared in this book are meant to grow with you, helping you navigate challenges, celebrate victories, and embrace the unique path that is yours to create. Every step forward is a testament to your strength and your commitment to living a life of authenticity, freedom, and joy.

If this book resonated with you or provided valuable guidance, I have a small favor to ask. Reviews are one of the best ways to help others discover books that can make a difference in their lives. If you found this book helpful, I would be so grateful if you could take a moment to leave a review on Amazon. Your honest feedback not only helps this book reach more readers but also inspires me and others to continue sharing ideas that encourage transformation and growth.

Thank you again for letting me be a part of your journey. I'm rooting for you as you move forward with courage, clarity, and purpose. The best is yet to come.

www.ingramcontent.com/pod-product-compliance
Lightning Source LLC
Chambersburg PA
CBHW071652240526
45469CB00021B/2091